Patterns and Relationships

Teaching early number in the National Curriculum

Marion H. Bird
Formerly Senior Lecturer in Mathematics: Chichester Institute of Higher Education (now University College: Chichester)

With a foreword by Professor Afzal Ahmed

Kingsham Press Limited
Chichester

First published 1999 by Kingsham Press Ltd
Chichester, West Sussex UK

British Library Cataloging in Publication Data
A catalogue record of the book is available from the British Library.

Bird, Marion

ISBN 0-9527912-1-8

ADDENDUM

During the lengthy publication process of the book, the National Numeracy Strategy has become a particular focus in schools. The fact that the activities suggested in the book have been analysed in terms of the National Curriculum for Mathematics (1995) rather than the National Numeracy Framework should in no way detract from their importance. It is immediately obvious from the Teaching Programme for key stages 1 and 2, that patterns and relationships in number are central to the whole National Numeracy Framework. Indeed, how could this be otherwise? Even the acquisition of efficient mental calculation strategies is dependent on children being able to make suitable connections and appreciate relationships.

Please note

Figures 1.3, 1.4 and 1.11 to 1.14 were originally meant to be printed in colour. The following brief notes should help with the interpretation of the black and white diagrams.

1.3 Starting from the 2nd section on the top right and going clockwise, the colours should be r r r r b r r r r b where r is red and b is blue.

1.4 The right hand side of the circle should be pink and the left hand side, blue.

1.11 The colours should be

g g p g g
p g g p g
g p g g p
g g p g g etc

1.12 The colours should be

g p g p g
p g p g p etc

1.13

p p g g p
p g g p p
g g p p g
g p p g g etc

1.14

g g g p g
g g p g g
g p g g g
p g g g p etc

in which g is for green and p is for purple.

Contents

Acknowledgements

I am particularly indebted to Afzal Ahmed from the Mathematics Centre of Chichester Institute of Higher Education (now University College: Chichester) for all his help and support.

I should also like to thank the following: Eira Gill for making me welcome at Woodcot County Primary School, Bridgemary, Hampshire, where she is the headteacher; Carolyn Watson, Alison Randall, Rebecca Dykes, Paul Johnson, Mary Talbot, Wendy Townrow and Lyndsay Bird for letting me work with their children and being interested in the activities; and John Mitchell for reading the drafts and making valuable comments.

Material from the National Curriculum is Crown copyright and is reproduced by permission of the Controller of HMSO. I am also grateful to Meryl Hargreaves and Yvonne Hughes for their permission to include the gridsheets shown in figure 2.4 which were taken from the Association of Teachers of Mathematics (1986) publication 10^2.

Foreword

In view of the current emphasis on numeracy and the enhanced focus on number work in schools, this book will be welcomed by teachers, teacher educators as well as parents.

Of all the subjects taught at school, mathematics continues to provoke the strongest negative emotions, often making pupils and teachers feel anxious and incompetent. The ever growing number of colourful pupil and teacher material does not appear to have alleviated this state to any significant extent. In this book, Marion goes to the core of Mathematics and pedagogy to tackle the mathematical confidence of young people. She does not offer direct recipes for action in the form of tips for teachers or a specific regime to be adhered to by teachers. Instead, she aims to strengthen the readers ability to make a substantial contribution in developing children's mathematical thinking.

Like an anthropologist, Marion has listened to young children and observed the simplicity and power with which they bring their native wit in tackling a range of problems. She combines these observations with exploiting the richness, fascination and intriguing connections that numbers can provide. The result is an invaluable treasure of suggestions and strategies which adults can employ to stimulate young children's mathematical thinking. The rich and comprehensive accounts of her work with young children of five and six years, enables readers to gain a clear insight in how to lay a firm foundation which will enable children to handle later work with confidence.

Patterns and relationship are at the heart of mathematics, but to date, little has been written about how to develop an awareness of such structure with younger age group children in schools. This book fills the gap that has existed for some time. It should be an essential read for all those concerned with education of young children.

Prof Afzal Ahmed, University College, Chichester

Sometimes a single unnamed child will be referred to as 'she' and sometimes as 'he'. This is to avoid clumsy expressions such as 'he/she' or 'his/her'.

Patterns and Relationships

Introduction

The emphasis on number

In the National Curriculum for Mathematics (1995), there is a great emphasis on number work for children in the early years. Indeed, number plays an even more prominent part than it did in earlier versions of the National Curriculum, with some of the previous topics being removed to create extra time and space for it.

Many people feel that this emphasis on number is appropriate for young children and it certainly fits in with the often heard plea for 'back to basics' in the classroom. But we need to ensure that 'the basics' are learnt in such a way as to be meaningful and readily retained, so that they do indeed provide a sound foundation on which the rest of a child's mathematics can be based.

Young children invariably start at school eager and curious, able to explore and initiate ideas, and these natural tendencies can be used constructively in the children's learning of mathematics. Although number work is particularly prone to being taught in a narrow, closed and uninspiring way, it is actually a tremendously rich source of fascination, with intriguing connections and patterns to be discovered and created. There is plenty of scope for young children's explorations, providing opportunities for children to ask some of their own questions and connect ideas together in a meaningful way. So it is possible to combine the 'Number' section of the Programme of Study for Mathematics in the National Curriculum with the active approach of the 'Using and Applying Mathematics' section, to give rise to purposeful and stimulating learning.

The underlying structure of number

With these points in mind, it is the main aim of this book to provide suggestions for activities which address items from the National Curriculum requirements for early number, whilst at the same time providing opportunities for the children to make and monitor decisions, develop mathematical language and communication, and develop mathematical reasoning as specified under the 'Using and Applying Mathematics' heading in the Programme of Study for Mathematics. The book is entitled 'Patterns and Relationships' because it concentrates particularly on the underlying structure of number, rather than on isolated facts and processes. Patterns and relationships are at the heart of everything in mathematics and an awareness of such structure in the early years can do much towards providing a firm foundation on which later work on number, algebra, shape, space, measures and handling data can grow.

Activities

The activities have been tried out with children in school and with teachers on in-service courses. A large number of examples of pupils' work are included in the book to give glimpses into children's handling of the ideas and the initiatives they have taken. Examples are included from across the whole five to eight years age range and the complete spectrum of abilities is represented. So that some of the examples can be set in a wider context, two case studies are included at the end of each chapter. Each case study describes how an activity was begun with children and continued for about half an hour.

Some of the ideas may already be familiar to teachers, but they have been included here to show how activities can be developed beyond work on the opening ideas themselves. Teachers often remark that one of their worries is that they are unsure of possible ways of encouraging the extension of starting-points and this has been borne in mind throughout the book. I would recommend that teachers try the activities themselves before working with children, so that they can obtain some awareness of the scope for generalisation etc. Having acquired such feel, however, it is important to try to keep an open mind to what actually happens with the children, so that artificial limits are not imposed.

Addressing the National Curriculum

Some statements in the Programme of Study for Number are clearly concerned with underlying structure and relationships, for example 'use repeating patterns to develop ideas of regularity and sequencing' (Key Stage 1, Number: 3a). In addressing such items, the activities suggested in this book also give rise to children participating in other items too: it seems to be inevitable that work on patterns etc. will involve other aspects of mathematics at the same time. Therefore much of the rest of the Programme of Study for Number will feature alongside the overt emphasis on structure. Moreover, some of the items from 'Shape, Space and Measures' will also feature. And, as indicated above, because of the active nature of the activities, many items are addressed from 'Using and Applying Mathematics' too.

There are also opportunities for links with other areas of the curriculum. As examples: (1) Discussing work and responding to and asking questions features significantly in the activities, hence aspects of English are included. Indeed, since there is an emphasis on children carrying out their own mathematical thinking, there is a built-in reason for communication through talking or writing: there is a point to the children explaining what they are doing. (2) Extensions of some activities, for instance the cross game in chapter 3, involve children in making their own designs. Patterning itself readily connects with many subjects other than mathematics and a range of cross-curricular suggestions is given at the end of chapter 1.

One way of covering the National Curriculum is, of course, to start with an item from the Programme of Study and devise a task centred around it and this is certainly how some of the ideas arose. To approach all of the National Curriculum in this way, however, is likely to be very restrictive, could make activities seem unrelated to one another, and gives little scope for encouraging and following up children's own ideas.

The alternative is to start with an activity which seems likely to stimulate children, see what happens when it is pursued and analyse the outcomes afterwards. This is how many of the activities now suggested in this book arose in the first place and this emphasis on activity first, then National Curriculum analysis later, is reflected in the structure of the chapters.

The National Curriculum analysis is carried out in terms of the Programme of Study for Key Stage 1. This is because the activities have been devised mainly with Key Stage 1 in mind and each of the detailed case studies is concerned with children from within that age-range. Because the activities provide for the whole range of abilities at Key Stage 1, however, there is considerable overlap with what is applicable to Key Stage 2. Obviously, many children up to some point of Key Stage 2 will have comparable abilities to some of the children within Key Stage 1. A few examples of work from children slightly older than the Key Stage 1 age-range have been included to serve as a reminder of that fact. It is also to be remembered that, because the activities have been written with an emphasis on providing opportunities for children to push forward their own thinking, there is much scope for differentiation by outcome and this reinforces the point about applicability to a range of different levels. It is also to be noted that the activities have been written to encourage all pupils to stretch themselves to their highest level of achievement.

The ideas and discussions are collected under five separate chapter headings: Early Patterning; Patterns in Number; Properties; Rules; and Missing Numbers. It is to be noted, however, that the topics interrelate, hence some ideas and points made under particular headings have links with other themes too.

Questions

As explained in the Introduction, each chapter ends with two case studies related to activities discussed in the text. Having read a case study, teachers might like to consider the following questions. Not all of these will be applicable to all the accounts, but they might comprise a useful reference list.

- What is suggested about individual children's ideas and understanding?
- Did the children set themselves any challenges? How did they participate in steering the activities?
- Which different aspects of the National Curriculum have been addressed?
- What might it be profitable to ask the children to do next? What would form a meaningful extension to the activity?
- At which points might different reactions from the children have altered what happened afterwards? How might the activity have proceeded differently?
- How do you think groups of children in your class would respond to the opening idea? How would it be best to phrase the starting-point for your children? How might the idea be embedded into an appropriate context for your class?

Chapter One: Early patterning

Given appropriate materials, young children often make patterns, including repeating patterns, spontaneously. As examples, Robert (3 years) joined large popping beads together so that there was one green, one pink, one green, one pink etc; and Ben (5 years) built up a line of plastic shapes in the order hexagon, trapezium, hexagon, trapezium etc. with a rhombus fitted in each of the angles created where the smaller of the parallel sides of the trapezia fitted onto the hexagons.

In the classroom, a teacher could focus attention on such instances through inviting a child who is building up a pattern to talk about what she is doing, or by asking other members of the group to say what they notice. Children could then be encouraged to make up more examples of their own.

Patterns with mistakes

Examples of non-patterns can be very helpful in trying to establish what a repeating pattern actually is. For example, a particular piece of wrapping paper, originally bought to wrap a child's birthday present, has become a treasured possession of mine. At first sight it looks as if there are lines of elephants arranged so that there is one brown one, followed by one grey one, followed by one brown one, followed by one grey one, and so on, but then closer observation reveals that there are two brown elephants together in the middle and one blue one at the end! Furthermore, there is a pattern to the bows round the elephants' necks and to the bows on the elephants' hats(!) which also break down in the middle and at one end.

Encouraging children to call out the colours in such a "pattern" can be useful in drawing their attention to the mistake. To continue with the wrapping paper example, a class of 5/6 year olds, looking along a line of the elephants, said together 'grey, brown, grey, brown, grey, brown ...', then there was confusion as some children said 'brown' (correctly) whilst others said 'grey', presumably influenced by continuing the pattern. Everybody stopped saying the colours. Several children made comments of surprise like 'Two browns!'; 'Two browns together: one there, one there!'; 'Two elephants brown, two elephants together!' All the children seemed amused by the situation and one announced 'There's a mistake.' The confusion created by different children calling out different colours served to focus the children's attention on looking closely at the arrangement, without any overt comments or questioning by the teacher.

The piece of wrapping paper was a particularly lucky find but, without such being available it is, of course, possible to make up one's own 'pattern' of a similar sort of nature, even simply with cubes of different colours or different sorts of geometric shapes etc. The idea that the teacher has made a mistake is very appealing to children!

As a follow up to discussing such a 'pattern', young children seem to delight in making up their own examples of patterns-with-mistakes. Other children can be encouraged to identify where the mistakes occur and what could happen to make the pattern correct. This is not always as simple to solve as might be thought at first and children can become really involved in grappling with the challenges presented. For example, given a strip of ducks as in figure 1.1, Carli (5 years) coloured them in brown (b) and green (g) from left to right as follows:

b g b g b b g g b b g b

This led to other 4/5 year olds in Carli's class wondering if the pattern had originally been 'one-one' (b, g, b, g, b, g etc.) or 'two-two' (b, b, g, g, b, b, g, g etc.) and it took a lot of thought to work out if and how those patterns could be re-established.

When devising examples of patterns with mistakes, some children find it helpful to build up a proper repeating pattern of cubes or counters in the chosen colours on top of the pictures (for example, the ducks) at first, then to switch round pairs of the cubes or counters or replace one by another colour etc.

Further activities and discussions could be developed around the following ideas. I have referred to 'ducks' for convenience but, obviously, any other pictures or objects could be used. These might be chosen to fit in with a current topic in which the class is involved, or perhaps a story could be woven round the situation.

(a) Ask children to look again at a pattern with a mistake in which they have decided that a particular pair of ducks has been switched. Is this the only possibility? Might two different ducks have been switched?

(b) Try asking children to switch two ducks which are in a pattern, then to switch them back again and switch two others. Do they think that the different switches give rise to the same sorts of mistakes or are they different?

(c) Having made a repeating pattern, children could be invited to try to make a different repeating pattern by switching pairs of the ducks. How many switches does it take?

Widening the scope

Whilst many children seem to enjoy devising repeating patterns, the construction or continuance of these per se, could become tedious after a while: not surprisingly tasks such as continuing 2, 1, 2, 1, 2, 1, 2, 1 ... are often seen as boring and pointless. It is possible, however, to devise activities which focus on the production of patterns but which incorporate some interesting challenges too and/or scope for a variety of other thinking processes as well. Some suggestions follow.

Figure 1.1

[A] A circle problem

Children can be asked to make up repeating patterns which fit round circular strips such as that shown in figure 1.2.

I have found it profitable to start such activities by colouring in a sequence of colours myself in front of the children which does not fit properly, for example two reds, three blues, two reds, three blues etc. As with the elephants example above, children seem intrigued by something-going-wrong and this often gives rise to spontaneous comments. For example, on one occasion when I had hurriedly coloured in the sequence of two reds, three blues ... in front of a group of 5/6 year olds, Michelle looked perturbed and came out with the delightful expression 'It's crashed!' Such perception of a problem naturally gives rise to the challenge 'Can a pattern be found which does work properly?'

Twelve is a particularly good number of regions to use since many patterns will fit this exactly. Once children have tried several examples, it might be profitable for them to list which patterns work and which do not and see if they can start to predict how other choices of patterns will behave.

There is scope for other conjectures to be made too. For example, Lindsey (5 years) thought that seven pinks would 'take up half'. Having seen someone else complete a six pink, six blue ... example, however, she realized that seven pinks, seven blue ... would be 'more than half' and added that seven pinks, six blues ... would not work either!

Children often seem to find a need to give a name to the regions in the strip and here is an opportunity for them to choose their own. On one occasion this led to a group of 5/6 year olds discussing whether 'oblong' was an appropriate name and how, in fact, oblongs were rather different because of their straight edges. They ended up with 'circle oblongs' which seemed very sensible.

It is interesting to see if any children create a series of patterns which are related to each other in some way. As examples, Louise (5 years) carried out three pinks, one blue ... for one pattern, followed by three blues, one pink ... for the next; and Katy (6 years) completed a pattern of one pink, one blue ..., followed by another two pinks, two blues, followed by a third of three pinks, three blues ... These children's growing awareness and use of structure are, perhaps, evidence of a particular facet of mathematical 'feel'. See Bird (1991), pp.102-8.

Two examples of children's work can be seen in figures 1.3 and 1.4. Natalie (6 years) had originally thought of attempting five pinks, five blues ... for this her third example, but when she tried it with counters she found it did not work. She then had the ingenious idea of using two sets of five pinks with one blue between them! Her writing is copied from my record of what she wanted to say about what she had done. Ricki (5 years) was amused by his six pinks, six blues ... result. His record of what he noticed is intended to read 'One side is pink - six. One side is blue - six.'

In the example discussed above, the children have used just two colours. The activity could, of course, be extended to use more colours, an idea which children might well think up themselves.

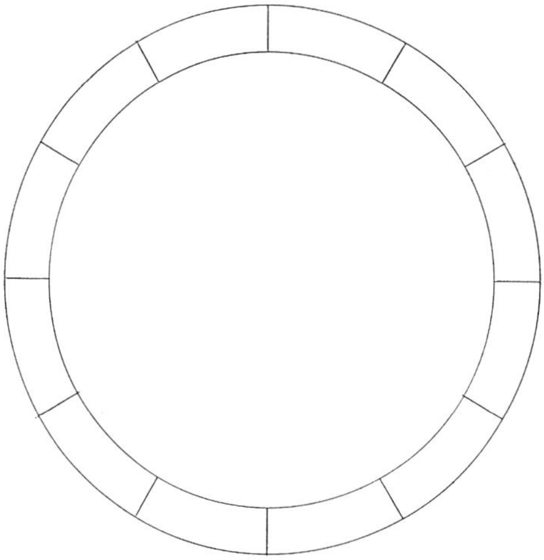

Figure 1.2

Figure 1.3

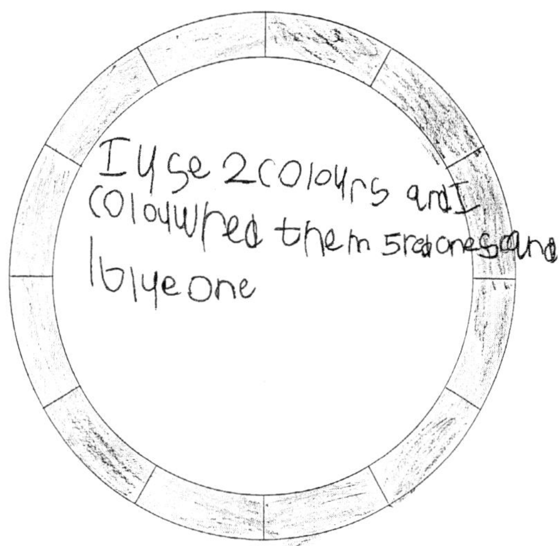

Figure 1.4

[B] Sets of patterns

Try asking children to make up a set of, say, three patterns underneath one another, perhaps using squares of coloured sticky paper.

This provides opportunities for children to construct patterns which are connected to one another in some way. For example, see figure 1.5 in which Ilona (5 years)

has started with	1 pink, 1 red, 1 yellow ...
then gone on to	2 pinks, 2 reds, 2 yellows ...
and continued with	3 pinks, 3 reds, 3 yellows ...

We might describe Ilona's work as devising some sort of structure and developing it.

Figure 1.5

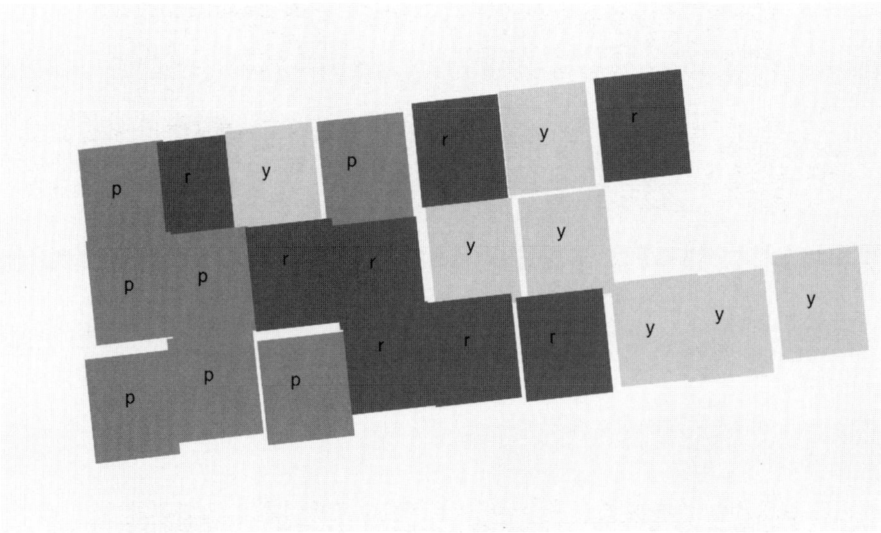

There is also scope for children to make connections between whole sets of their patterns. For example, Rachel (5 years) seemed not only to devise and vary a theme within her first set of three patterns (see figure 1.6), she also developed the theme in her second set of three patterns (see figure 1.7). See Bird (1991), pp.141-4 for further discussions of similar examples.

Children could be asked questions about how their, or other children's, patterns would continue. They might also be encouraged to think whether it would be possible to add any more patterns to their sets. For example, is it possible to add another line to Rachel's work shown in either figure 1.6 or 1.7? If a child thinks that he could not do so, he could be asked how he can be certain. Gropings towards an awareness of impossibility can form early and important experience of some of the underlying principles of mathematical proof.

Figure 1.6

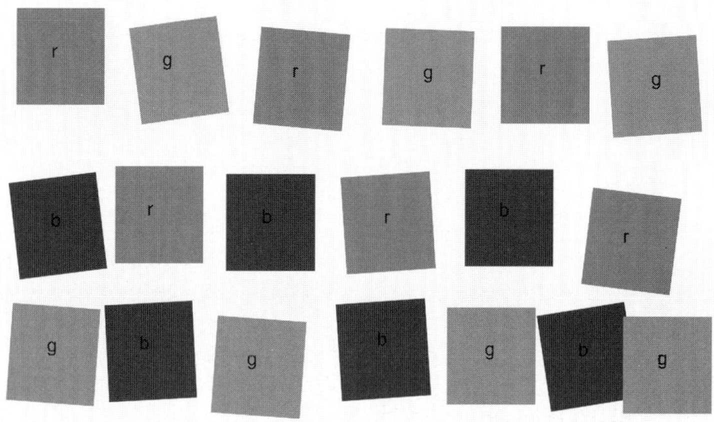

Figure 1.7

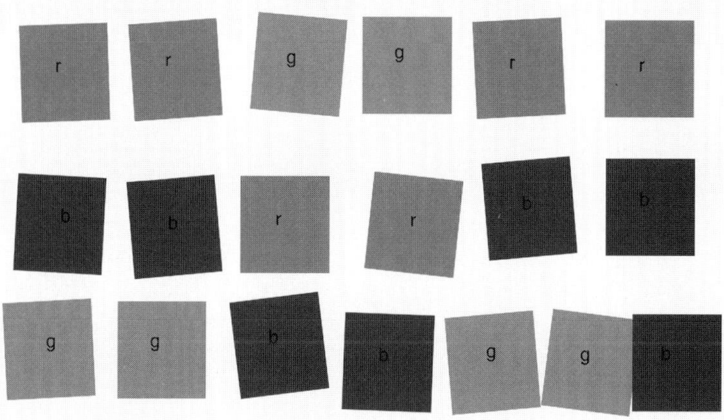

[C] From one dimension to two dimensions

Ask children to make a repeating pattern along a strip of squares, for example as in figure 1.8, children could be asked to copy a pattern onto a rectangle so that they go along the top line from left to right, then continue the pattern on the next line again starting from the left hand end, and so on. In that way, the pattern shown in figure 1.8 yields the pattern shown in figure 1.9 when transferred to a five by twelve rectangle.

It sometimes helps with the procedure of transferring the patterns, if children work in pairs with one child looking along the strip calling out each colour to be used and the other child colouring in the squares on the rectangle.

Children often notice other patterns arising in their rectangles. They can be encouraged to think whether and how these patterns would continue.

Having completed a rectangle, children could be asked which horizontal lines are the same and whether they notice anything about when these happen. They could also see how many different horizontal lines they can find. Particular features could be looked for in lines, for example, symmetry.

The pattern two reds, two blues ... simply produces vertical blocks of colours on, say, an eight by ten rectangle. It is interesting to find other rectangles for which this is the case. For a given rectangle, children could also inquire into which strip patterns give rise to this sort of block pattern.

Another idea for consideration is for children to find the largest patch of one single colour on their rectangles. How many squares does this take up? Could they make patterns which produce even larger patches?

A case study of children working on the activity is included at the end of this chapter.

Figure 1.8

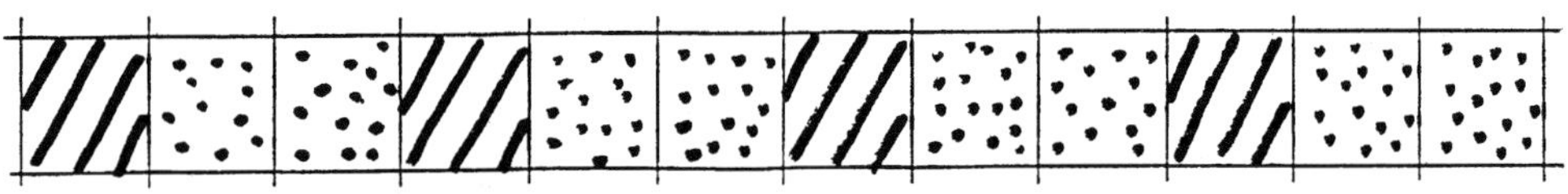

Figure 1.9

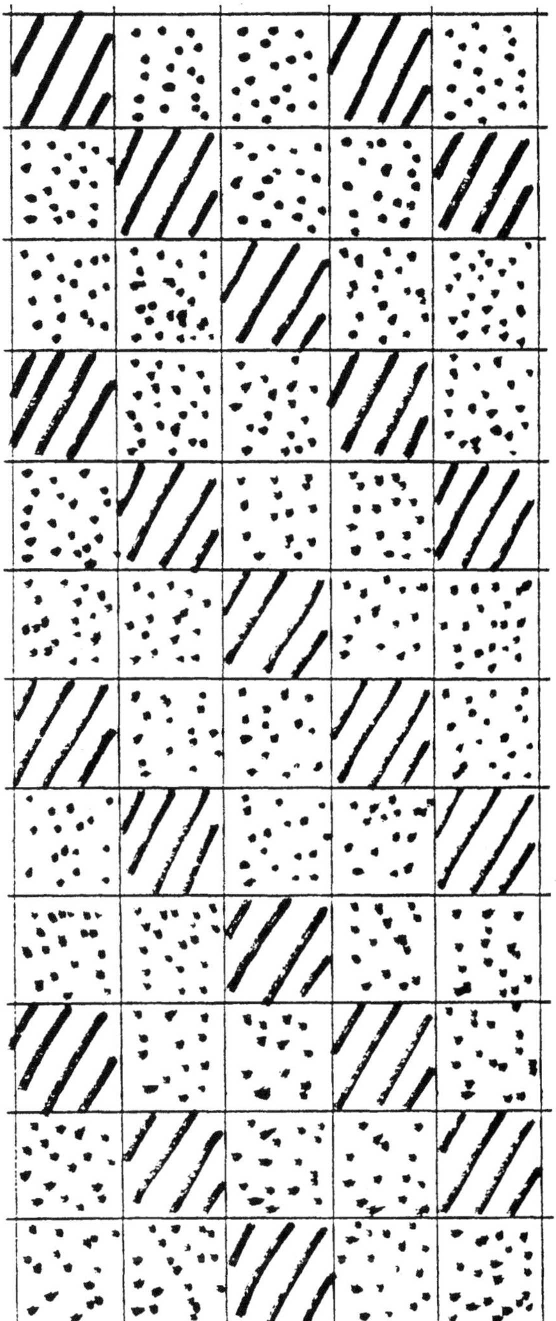

[D] Holding squares of coloured card

Give each group of children a coloured square of card to hold in front of them and ask other children arrange the group so that they make a pattern.

For a given number of children with a particular colour of card each, quite a small number of patterns are likely to be possible. For example, suppose four children are given a piece of green card (g) and four children are given a piece of yellow card (y), then the following are all right

y g y g y g y g
g y g y g y g y
y y g g y y g g
g g y y g g y y

but something like y y y g repeated will not work, for even though the repetition of the sequence would take up exactly eight children, it would demand more children holding yellow than are available. Children could be involved in deciding exactly how many repeating patterns are possible for a given combination of colours within a given number of children. The likely smallness of the number means that attention could be paid to considering how the children can be certain no more solutions can be found. Alternatively, for a choice of pattern which does not work, children could try to determine (a) how many changes of colour would be necessary amongst the given line of children, and (b) if extra children would be needed to make the sequence end tidily.

In cases such as (b), children with some knowledge of numbers over ten could be involved in finding more than one solution. For example, with a two yellow, three green ... pattern with twelve children, either another 3 children, or 8 children, or 13 children, or 18 children could be used as extras to make sure the sequence is complete. These numbers themselves could be investigated with scope for further pattern-spotting and predictions etc.

Suppose the line of children has been arranged successfully by a child so that the cardboard squares are in a pattern. When another child decides on a different pattern, questions can be asked such as 'What is the smallest number of children who need to change places?' 'Who needs to move where?'

A case study of children working on the activity is included at the end of this chapter.

Colour blindness

Colour plays an important role in a lot of patterning activities. For children suffering from some forms of colour blindness, this could present a problem. One alternative is to use geometric shapes in place of colours. For recording purposes, templates of shapes could be used if the children are adept enough at handling these, or activities could be centred on using little gummed shapes (stars, bells etc.) which are easily available.

In any case, it seems sensible for all children to experience a variety of ways of patterning, so work with geometric shapes etc. should be valuable for all.

THE NATIONAL CURRICULUM FOR KEY STAGE 1 MATHEMATICS

All the activities discussed so far centre on requiring pupils to 'recognise simple patterns and relationships and make related predictions about them' (Using and Applying Mathematics: 4a) and to 'use repeating patterns to develop ideas of regularity and sequencing' (Number: 3a).

There is also a lot of scope for pupils to 'discuss their work, responding to and asking mathematical questions'; to 'ask questions including "What would happen if?" and "Why?"'; and to 'explain their thinking to support the development of their reasoning' (Using and Applying Mathematics: 3c, 4b and 1b respectively).

Devising patterns will necessitate some awareness of simple number, including counting small numbers, as in Number: 2a.

Other Key Stage 1 topics may well feature in particular activities. As examples:

> Children are likely to use words such as 'next to', 'before' etc. when describing their patterns and how to move colours etc. This will involve them in Using and Applying Mathematics: 3a.
>
> Activities for which some patterns will work but others will not, could involve children in sorting and classifying as in Number: 5a, also in collecting, recording and interpreting data as in Number: 5b.
>
> Activities which use shapes in the formation of patterns are likely to involve children in the recognition and naming of simple shapes and in familiarising them with simple properties of shapes. This links with Shape, Space and Measures: 2.
>
> Activities such as 'A circle problem' (p 9) may well involve children in thinking about the meaning of the word 'half' as in Number: 2c.
>
> Some of the activities lead to involvement in solving a problem, for example in the 'Holding squares of coloured card' activity (p 14) when children try to find exactly how many repeating patterns are possible for a given combination of colours within a given number of children. This provides opportunities for children to 'use and apply mathematics in practical tasks, in real-life problems and within mathematics itself' (Using and Applying Mathematics: 1a).

Across the curriculum

The ideas in this chapter for activities on repeating patterns, could be incorporated into a wider project on patterning. Within mathematics, an appropriate extension would be to consider symmetry, both in terms of children recognizing and exploring what we would term 'line symmetry' and 'rotational symmetry'. Tessellation is another interesting area in which patterning plays an essential part.

The topic could also spread right across the curriculum. The suggestions below are just a few of many possible ideas:

Examine and describe repeating patterns in wallpaper, wrapping-paper, fabrics, porcelain etc. Design, say, a piece of patterned wrapping-paper to use at Christmas. The work on fabrics could be viewed cross-culturally, with reference to ancient civilisations too.

Print patterns, for example, with potato prints.

Find and explore patterns in nature: look at honeycombs, fir-cones, feathers etc.

Find and take rubbings of different types of brick patterns. Look for and describe different tiling patterns.

Make up a series of connected movements (for example, roll, stand up, jump), and keep repeating the sequence. Make up a sequence for someone else to try.

Make up and repeat simple rhythms. Make up and repeat patterns of varying sounds, for example stamp, stamp, clap, clap, clap. Repeat sequences of notes on chime bars etc.

Learn and practise handwriting patterns.

Find and learn how to spell words with particular patterns of letters in them.

Find patterns of rhyming words in poetry.

Read stories and poems with sets of repeating patterns of words in them (for example, 'The shopping basket' by John Burningham, published by Picture Lions).

Some activities which at first seem specifically connected with one area of the curriculum might well lead to other areas too. For example, see figure 1.10 for an example of how an activity, started in a music session, led to some interesting mathematics.

The book 'Mathematics through art and design 6 - 13' by Anne Woodman and Eric Albany, published by Collins, 1988, contains many helpful ideas. The Project File on 'Pattern' in November 1991 issue of Child Education (Volume 68, Number 11) is also a very useful resource, as is the January 1991 issue of Strategies: Maths and problem solving 3 - 13 (Volume 1, Number 3) which is devoted to the theme of 'pattern'.

Figure 1.10

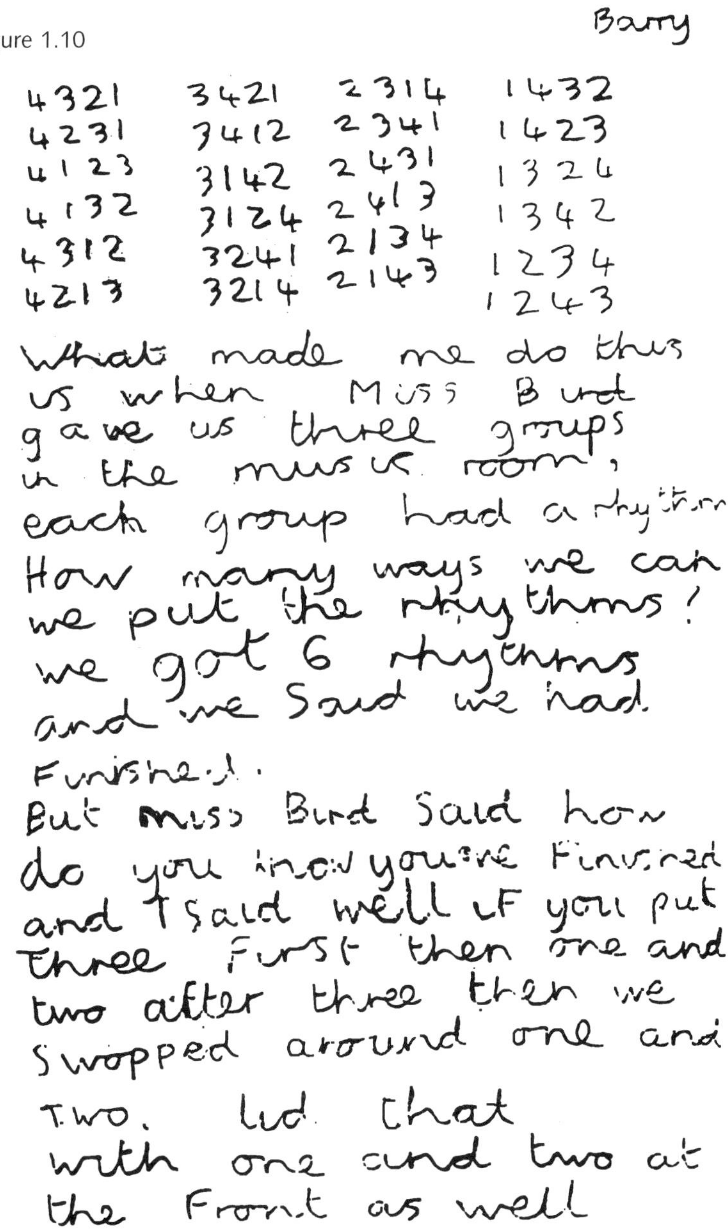
Barry

4321	3421	2314	1432
4231	3412	2341	1423
4123	3142	2431	1324
4132	3124	2413	1342
4312	3241	2134	1234
4213	3214	2143	1243

What made me do this us when Miss Bird gave us three groups in the music room, each group had a rhythm How many ways we can we put the rhythms? we got 6 rhythms and we said we had finished. But miss Bird said how do you know you're finished and I said well if you put three first then one and two after three then we swopped around one and two. Did that with one and two at the front as well

Figure 1.10 cont.

Then miss Bird Said
would you like to see
How many ways can
set it out using 4123?
I Found out the answer
it was 24
The reason why I Know
There's no more is
because I put Four in
Front then I put three
then I put Two and one
then I Swopped 2 and 1
around Like this 4321
I did the Same 4312
with the
numbers
4231 4132
4213 4123
then I put three in the
Front 3421 3241 3124
3412 3214 3142
I did this with one and
two at the Front as well.

Case study: From one dimension to two dimensions

I showed a group of four 6 year olds a strip of twelve squares, took a green and purple pencil and quickly coloured in the squares in front of them: one green, two purple, one green, two purple etc. They commented on it being a pattern and read it out in terms of the numbers of greens and purples as I have just written.

Giving each of the children a strip of twelve squares and a green and a purple pencil, I invited them to make a pattern too and said that perhaps they could make theirs different from mine. I added that I had rushed the colouring of my strip but that they need not do so. They set about the task eagerly, Daniel choosing for his pattern two green, one purple; Katy two purple, two green; Charlene three greens, one purple; and Stuart one green, one purple. Hence, whether by design or accident, they each chose a pattern which was not only different from mine, but different from each other's also. They coloured in their strips unaided, taking much more care than I had done. Indeed, Stuart was so slow and meticulous that I wondered if he would ever finish.

Katy was the first to complete her strip. I commented that she was now going to use her pattern to do something else. I took out a rectangular piece of squared paper, five squares by twelve, and placed it in front of her with the shorter side going across the table. I invited her to try to copy her pattern on this set of squares, starting across the top five squares then continuing across the next five squares and so on, going from left to right each time. She coloured purple, purple, green, green, purple across the top, then hesitated. I asked her what came next in her pattern to which she replied 'another purple'. I pointed to where that purple should go at the left hand end of the next line (under the first purple square) and she was then quite happy to continue. The others appeared to have listened to the explanation as well and, although they each wanted to show me their strips when they had finished them, they seemed confident how to proceed on the five by twelve squares.

The children were able to continue on their own. I was surprised that they coped with the ends and beginnings of lines so well as I had thought that keeping the pattern going might prove quite difficult. As they coloured in more and more squares, they were excited to find more patterns forming and this gave much scope for observations and predicting how the new designs would continue.

Having completed three horizontal lines, Daniel thought there was going to be a pattern of green, purple, green, purple etc. down the left hand side of his rectangle. Once he had coloured in a few more lines, however, he realized that he needed to change his idea. He said 'I thought it was going to be a one pattern but it's one, one, two, one, two, one, two, one, two .' Then, thinking ahead about where the colours would go he added 'but it will end up like that bit' showing that it would end with a single green like it had started with a single green, whereas there were two greens together each time in the middle. See figure 1.11 for Daniel's completed pattern.

Figure 1.11

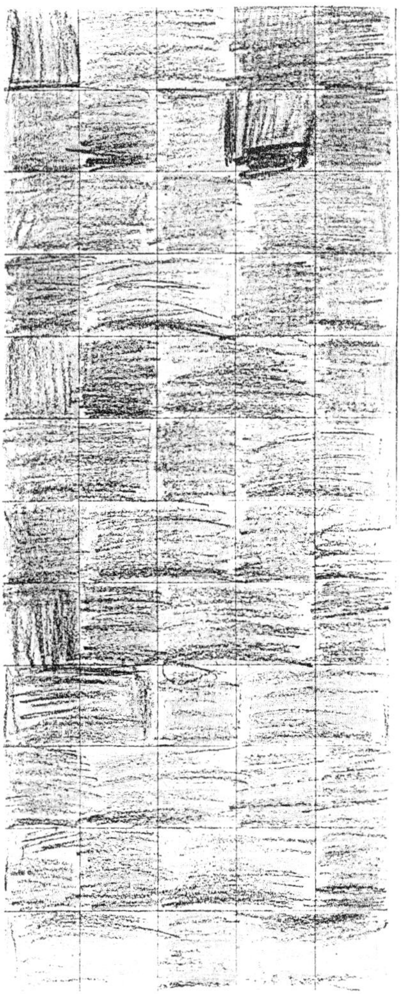

Figure 1.12

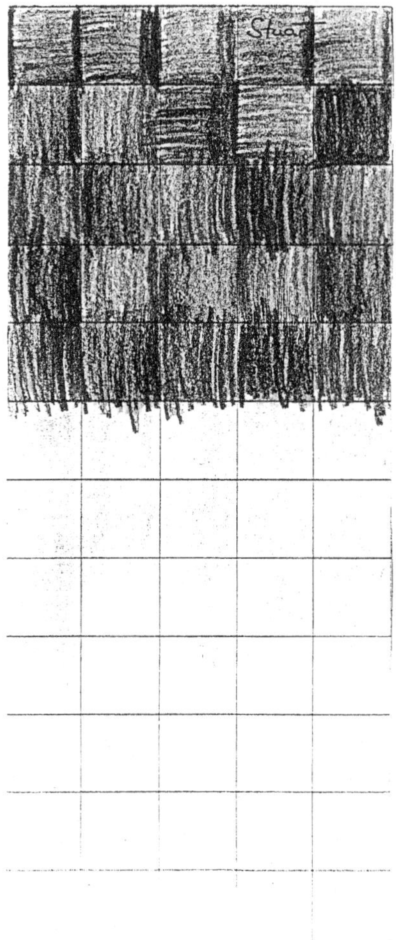

Stuart was excited to find that, down the left hand side of his page, exactly the same pattern was forming as he had chosen originally. He said 'It's sort of green, purple, green, purple, green. It's the same going across.' See figure 1.12 for Stuart's pattern. Because of his painstaking colouring, he did not have time to complete his rectangle.

As Katy was colouring in her paper she exclaimed 'It's a staircase! It goes diagonal!' Then she realized that there were in fact two different coloured 'staircases' and pointed out 'It goes purple, green, purple, green', drawing her finger along the appropriate diagonal line of colour each time. See figure 1.13 for Katy's pattern.

Figure 1.13

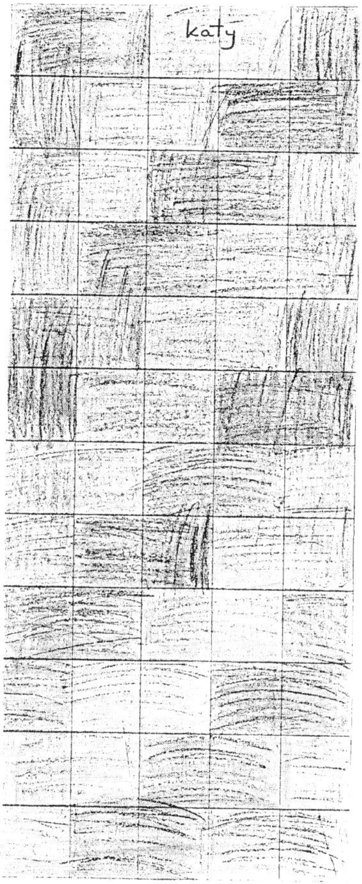

Figure 1.14

Charlene also discovered a staircase in the start of her pattern. She was referring to the top purple diagonal line as shown in figure 1.14. As her colouring progressed, she was excited to find more of them forming too. Daniel discovered one in his rectangle as well. This was going in the opposite direction to Charlene's but he did not comment on that. Noticing that there were in fact several unconnected diagonal purple lines, he added 'There's a giant staircase broke up' (sic) and pointed out a green staircase between the purple lines. I asked how this green staircase was different from the purple one and he explained 'Because it's got two going down.'

Several children commented on features of individual horizontal lines. For example, drawing attention to her fourth line down, Charlene said 'It's purple, green, green, green, purple.' She did not mention this pattern occurring on the ninth line too, but she was delighted to find that the rectangle actually ended with that arrangement.

Case study: Holding squares of coloured card

To each of twelve children from a class of 5/6 year olds, I gave a piece of coloured card. Six children had red pieces and six had blue. The remaining children were to act as 'organizers', taking it in turn to arrange the twelve children so that their cards formed a pattern.

I asked Andrew to organize the group first. He called out the twelve children in turn in the order blue, red, blue, red etc. I suggested the children made a line at the front of the class, facing the rest.

Whilst they were lining themselves up, two children muddled their positions with the result that two blues and two reds ended up together. This gave

b r b r b r b b r r b r (1)

instead of b r b r b r b r b r b r (2)

Carli spotted the two blues together and told James, who was holding the red card at the end of the line, to go between the two blues. This gave

b r b r b r b r b r r b (3)

Lindsey saw that that still left two reds together. She suggested that Claire, who was holding one of the two adjacent reds, should 'go at the end next to a blue'. This gave the correct sequence. Together we called out the pattern which Andrew had originally chosen.

Christopher was next to organize the group. He said he wanted to do 'red, blue, red, blue ...'. This, of course, was still a one-one pattern like the first example, but starting with the opposite colour. I asked if he could see a way of changing everybody quickly. He thought for a moment then switched each pair of children around in turn. He said things like 'Toby and David swop places', 'Kelly and Rebecca change'. After each pairwise swop, two children holding the same colour were momentarily left side by side. Some of these children objected until they realized Christopher was going to swop one of them with the next person in any case. This ripple of discontent moved down the line until the process was complete! Of course it would have been difficult for the children actually in the line to be aware of Christopher's overall plan. At the end, Lindsey commented that there had been blue at the beginning (in Andrew's arrangement) and now there was blue at the end.

Carli wanted to do 'blue, blue, red, red ...'. She said she would 'get two reds together and two blues together'. With Lindsey's help she moved the children round competently and completed the pattern very quickly.

Lee was eager to have a go next. Instead of choosing a new pattern he wanted to go back to the original one. He moved the first four children correctly, but then ended up with rather a pickle, that is

b r b r r b r b r b b r (4)

Sorting this out took quite some time with a number of children totally engrossed in arguing with one another and often trying to reason ahead what would happen. For example, starting from (4), Lee wanted to switch round the fifth child (red) with the sixth (blue) and the seventh (red) with the eighth (blue) but Charlene saw that this would still give two reds together.

Eventually the line was sorted out. Before continuing, it seemed sensible to involve the children in recapping on the patterns which had been used so far. Lindsey mentioned the red, blue, red, blue ... one; Andrew the blue, red, blue, red ... one; and Natalie blue, blue, red, red ... I asked if anyone could think of a different arrangement. Natalie said we could have a 'three pattern'. She arranged Ricki, David and Lindsey together (all reds), followed by Scott, Toby and James (all blues); Charlene, Rebecca and Claire (reds); and Louise, Angela and Kelly (blues). Angela was quite distressed: she kept on emphasizing that there were three blues at the end. Carli explained, 'That's how Natalie wanted it.' Angela, however, still seemed convinced that something was wrong. Further probing revealed that she thought there were only two blues at the other end. Natalie could see the problem: Scott was standing slightly behind the children adjacent to him and could not be seen by Angela. Once Scott had stood forward and we called out all the colours in order, Angela seemed content.

Natalie was eager to try another example. She wanted to do a 'four pattern'. Although she had already had a go, I made a quick decision to let her continue. Because of the structuring implicit in the sequence of patterns, it seemed worthy of emphasis that we had had a two pattern and a three pattern and were now trying a four pattern. Also, a four pattern would be impossible with just six of each colour available, and it would be interesting to gain glimpses into the children's awareness of the problem.

Natalie chose four children with blue cards and four children with red and arranged them in a line. She did not say anything about the two remaining blues and reds. I asked if she were going to do anything with the children left over. She placed them at the right hand end giving

b b b b r r r r b b r r (5)

Several children were indignant: it was not right! Lindsey suggested that the two pairs could go 'at the other end' but Carli realized that that would not help. David announced, 'It's a mistake!' He had been involved in the ducks activity earlier (see p.)! I asked if we could do anything about the 'mistake'. Lindsey was still insistent that the two pairs 'could go at the other end.' I decided to let her try this. Then she herself realized that it did not work. Mark exclaimed, 'There are not enough!'

It seemed appropriate to try to involve the children in grappling with Mark's perception further. I asked all the children with blue cards to stand together. I counted out four of them and asked how many children were left. Then I repeated the process a couple of times for different combinations of four children. I asked, 'Is there any way we can choose them so we are left with more than two?' The class seemed sure that there was not. I commented that although we could start a four, four pattern, then, we could not go very far with it unless we involved more children with red and blue cards.

By this time, we had been working on the patterning for about twenty-five minutes. It did not seem appropriate to go through any more examples practically as some of the children were starting to fidget. I mentioned this to the group but added that, if anyone still had any more ideas, they could say what they were and they could be tried out on another occasion.

Natalie immediately offered 'six and six'. Wondering what her response would be I asked, 'Why didn't you say five and five?' She said it would not work 'because there would be one left'. Presumably she meant one of each colour, like we had had two of each colour left with the four and four pattern. Carli added that there would be 'two left at the end'. It was interesting to note these two girls' growing facility with number bonds. Natalie's mother happened to be in the classroom at the time and said afterwards that she was amazed at her daughter's capabilities.

Andrew suggested 'eight and nine' as another pattern! Carli quickly told him 'We haven't got enough' and Lindsey explained 'Six and six is twelve. We'd need more colours.'

Lee suggested putting 'all the blues in a line and all the reds in a line'. Natalie commented that that was like the six and six idea.

No more suggestions were forthcoming at that point, but Michelle told me later in the day that she had had another idea: two reds and one blue! This was the first example of a pattern in which the number of reds and blues were not the same. Trying this out with the children on another occasion could certainly open up the potential of the exploration further.

Chapter Two: Patterns in number

'Number' featured in the examples in the previous chapter since the patterns consisted of particular numbers of colours, shapes etc. being repeated. In this chapter, however, the focus is more overtly on numbers themselves: it is concerned with patterns within numbers, not patterns formed from other objects.

Our number system is a tremendously rich source of interesting patterns. Indeed, it is rare not to come up with a pattern when carrying out explorations within number.

Simple addition patterns

Number patterns can be generated simply through continuous addition. Children can be asked to choose a number, then add a number to it, then keep on adding that number to the last one formed. So, starting with 12, say, and continuously adding 5 one obtains

12, 17, 22, 27, 32, 37 ...

which has a repeating pattern in the units.

If several children are working on this activity at once, it might be sensible to encourage them all to add on the same number each time, but to choose their own starting numbers. Then there is scope for them to become involved in comparing patterns and seeing which starting numbers yield the same patterns. Further possibilities are for them to predict the next few terms in their sequences, then to see if they are correct; also, to think if/why they are certain that the patterns will continue. Having discussed as a group the set of patterns obtained for adding on a particular number each time, it would be interesting for individuals to choose their own number for the repeated addition and explore the patterns created.

A case study of children working on a repeated addition activity is included at the end of this chapter. It is to be noted that these children used calculators to produce their number chains. To have spent time working out each addition is likely to have detracted from the overall activity. Often the use of a calculator can free children to concentrate on processes such as pattern-spotting, making conjectures and generalizing. This is not to argue that calculators should always be used and that children need not practise mental arithmetic - far from it - but to point out that calculators have a very important part to play in parts of mathematics, work on early algebra being one of them.

Tables patterns

Some repeated addition patterns give rise, of course, to the 'answers' of what are recognized as 'multiplication tables'. Thus, starting at 3 (or 0) and adding on in threes gives the results of the 3 x table, that is the multiples of 3.

However children are introduced to the different multiplication tables (and here is not the place to discuss such introduction), tables constitute a rich source of patterns, a fact which is no doubt familiar to everybody reading this book. Often activities are restricted to spotting patterns within the simple tables from 1 to 10, but there is much more potential than this.

Consider, for example, figure 2.1. Claire, aged 6/7, had chosen to investigate the patterns in the 2 x table. She worked out the numbers in her head from 2 to 64 and saw that the units kept on repeating, as can be seen from her comment towards the middle of the page. I suggested she then tried the 12 x table, this time using a calculator. She quickly saw that she obtained the same pattern in the units, though this time she did not make a note of that observation. She then decided that the 22 x table would probably behave in the same way and set about testing her prediction, also guessing at two of the numbers (66 and 88) en route. Having found that the same pattern did indeed emerge, she was able to state with confidence which other tables would also act the same. It would have been interesting to have seen if she could explain why these particular tables produced the same pattern.

Figure 2.1

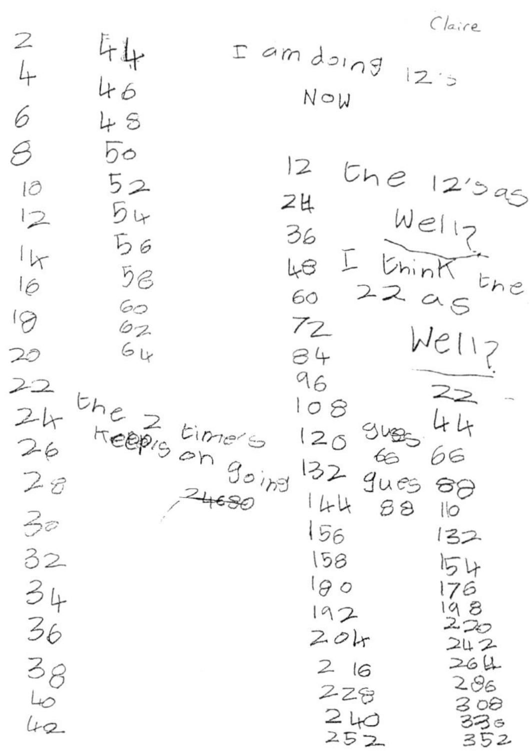

Sometimes children observe patterns in the tens as well as or instead of patterns in the units. For example, Rebecca, aged 6/7, was excited to notice a pattern in the tens of the 3 x table, namely that there were

three 1s (12, 15, 18), three 2s (21, 24, 27), four 3s (30, 33, 36, 39)

followed by

three 4s (42, 45, 48), three 5s (51, 54, 57), four 6s (60, 63, 66, 69)

and so on.

Children can be encouraged to look at where the answers to some tables appear within other ones. For example, circling round the 4 x table answers in the 2 x table gives the following:

2468101214161820 ...

This provides more opportunities for pattern-spotting, conjecturing, reasoning, generalizing etc.

Similarly, children can be asked to carry out some operation on each of the numbers in a table and to see what happens. For example, they could be asked to double the numbers in different tables. Children often find it exciting to discover that this gives rise to other tables. It is an important discovery and its significance needs emphasising so that children can appreciate that, given knowledge of one multiplication table, they can use it to produce other number facts which they have not yet committed to memory.

Once table patterns have been discovered by children, these themselves can be worked on further. For example, it could be pointed out that if we start with the table pattern 0 2 4 6 8, add 4 to each of the numbers and look at just the units, one ends up with 4 6 8 0 2, which can be thought of as the same pattern and is easily seen as such if the numbers are written in a cycle:

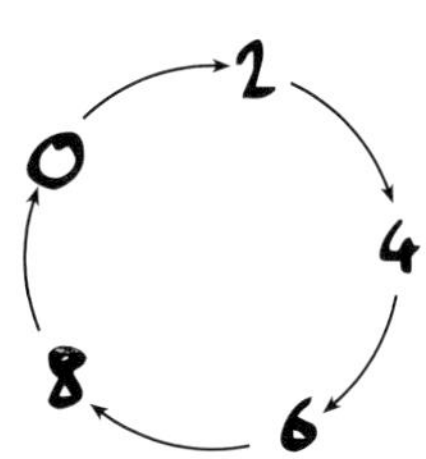

This then begs the question: which other additions can be carried out on the numbers, to end up with the same pattern?

For children who are starting to become confident with simple division, a further interesting activity is to start with a particular multiplication table and then find the remainders when each of the numbers in that table is divided by a particular number. For example, suppose we start with the numbers from the 2 x table and find the remainders on division by 3 for each of the numbers:

2÷3 = 0 r2;   4÷3 = 1 r1;   6÷3 = 2 r0;   8÷3 = 2 r2 etc.

Writing out the remainders under the numbers in the 2 x table gives an interesting pattern:

2	4	6	8	10	12	14	16	18	20
⇓	⇓	⇓	⇓	⇓	⇓	⇓	⇓	⇓	⇓
2	1	0	2	1	0	2	1	0	2

What happens with other tables? And with other divisors?

A variety of 1 - 100 square type grids

Teachers often make use of the 1 to 100 square to provide a fund of patterns for children to find. One common example is for children to colour in the numbers from different multiplication tables (viewed perhaps in a 'counting on' sense) and to see what patterns emerge. Opportunities for prediction are easily provided: having coloured in several numbers, children can be asked think ahead which number will be coloured next.

A potentially rich extension to this idea is to keep to the same rule for which particular numbers are to be coloured, but to vary the number of columns in the grid. 1 to 100 squares normally, of course, have ten columns but there is no need to keep to this. So, for example, a five column grid would appear as in figure 2.2. Try colouring every third number on different grids. What happens? For which numbers of columns do the patterns look similar to one another? Why do you think they are similar? Which numbers of columns give rise to vertical line patterns? Why does that happen?

Figure 2.3 shows three 7/8 year old children's work on circling numbers in the 2 x table in grids with different numbers of columns. The children seemed particularly intrigued by the pattern which Rebecca referred to as a 'chessboard'. Other children described this pattern in other ways, for example, Simon said it looked like 'patchwork'. When choosing different grids, gradually the children became aware that their patterns were of only two different sorts, the sort just mentioned and vertical lines. See Bird (1986), Chapter 4, for more details. There is potential here for children to see which numbers of columns yield which sorts of patterns, to reason why this is so, and to start to predict what would happen with other numbers of columns. See the case study at the end of chapter 3 for a more detailed account of similar work with younger children.

Figure 2.2

1	2	3	4	5
6	7	8	9	10
11	12	13	14	15
16	17	18	19	20
21	22	23	24	25
26	27	28	29	30
31	32	33	34	35
36	37	38	39	40

Figure 2.3

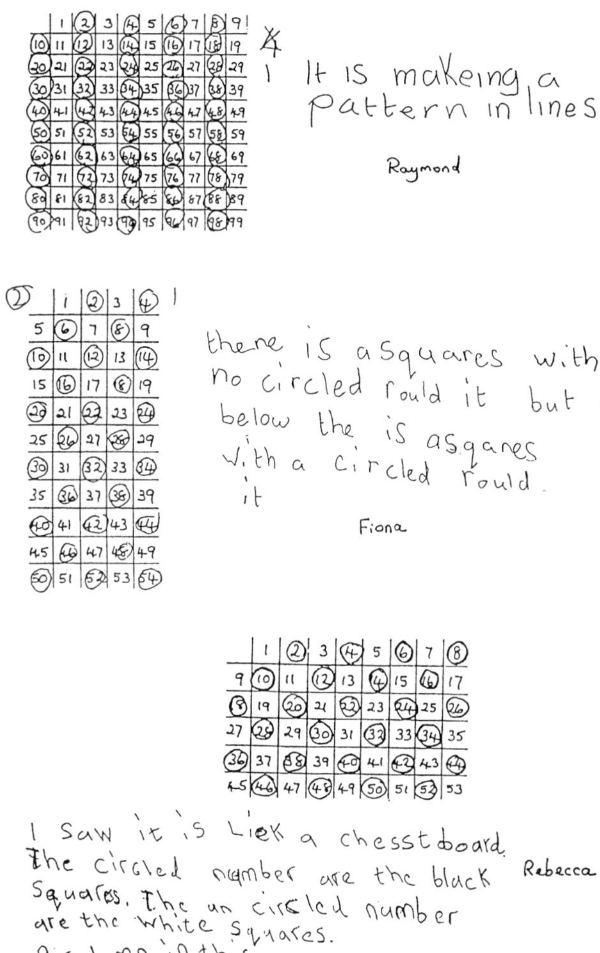

Calendars are a useful and interesting source of seven column number grids. Work on number patterns within these could perhaps be part of a more general topic on time.

Here are three more activities which seem particularly fruitful with 1 - 100 type grids:

[A] Take any line...

Invite children to choose a line of numbers on a grid. The line can be where they like, going in any direction and containing as many numbers as they please. What can the children say about the numbers in their chosen line? 1

Asking children to describe to other children the patterns they can see in the numbers in their chosen lines and seeing if these other children can identify the lines, proves to be an enjoyable and challenging activity for many children.

[B] Adding numbers from particular columns

Ask children each to choose two columns on a grid. Then they are to pick a number from one of these columns and a number from the other column and add them together. They are to keep repeating the process for the same two columns. What do they notice about the answers?

If children use grids with ten columns they are likely to notice that the units of the answers they obtain are always the same. For other grids, a variety of units may well occur in the answers but then it is interesting to see in which columns the answers lie on the grids (as indeed it is with ten-column grids too).

If the answer which is obtained from a pair of numbers is beyond the end of the grid, this begs the question, if the grid is extended, in which column will the answer lie?

There are opportunities for children to impose a particular order on the way in which they select numbers from the columns. This is likely to give way to further patterning. For example, suppose

the 1st	number in the 3rd column	is added to the	1st	number in the 8th column;
" 2nd	—— " ——	—— " ——	3rd	—— " ——
" 3rd	—— " ——	—— " ——	5th	—— " ——
" 4th	—— " ——	—— " ——	7th	—— " ——
" 5th	—— " ——	—— " ——	9th	—— " ——

then this produces

$$
\begin{aligned}
1 + 7 &= 8 \\
11 + 27 &= 38 \\
21 + 47 &= 68 \\
31 + 67 &= 98 \\
41 + 87 &= 128
\end{aligned}
$$

There is a difference of 30 between each adjacent pair of the numbers obtained. Some high attaining children may well be able to spot such patterns or at least recognize that the 'tens go up in threes'. They could try to explain why this common difference occurs.

Pupils may well find that two sums give them the same answer. For example, 21 + 57 would be the same as 11 + 67. They could be asked to think why this happens.

A case study of children working on the activity is included at the end of this chapter.

[C] Squares within grids

Ask children to choose a small square of four numbers from within the usual ten column 1 - 100 square, for example

13 14
23 24

Now they are to add up the numbers on the diagonals, that is

13 + 24 = 37
14 + 23 = 37.

What happens with other squares? Is the answer always the same? Can you think why this happens?

Even if they start off cautiously by choosing squares in the top left hand corner of the grid, children often choose what they see as 'hard' squares eventually. This can provide a lot of practice in addition involving the exchange of units for tens. If coping with such arithmetic is likely to detract from the overall activity, calculators could be used of course.

Asked for suggestions of how to develop the idea, children might suggest trying larger squares, or different shapes such as rectangles, or subtraction instead of addition. As with the other activities, it is also fruitful to consider grids comprising other numbers of columns.

There is scope for investigating the totals themselves. For example, the totals for the diagonals in the 2 x 2 squares, placed without overlaps, along the top two lines of a 1 - 100 square are 13, 17, 21, 25, 29. These go up in fours. Why?

Other grids

Other arrangements of numbers in grids are possible of course. The ATM Activity book "10^2" contains some interesting gridsheets, two examples of which are shown in figure 2.4. These provide a fund of further possibilities for pattern spotting.

Figure 2.4

73	74	75	76	77	78	79	80	81	82
72	43	44	45	46	47	48	49	50	83
71	42	21	22	23	24	25	26	51	84
70	41	20	7	8	9	10	27	52	85
69	40	19	6	1	2	11	28	53	86
68	39	18	5	4	3	12	29	54	87
67	38	17	16	15	14	13	30	55	88
66	37	36	35	34	33	32	31	56	89
65	64	63	62	61	60	59	58	57	90
100	99	98	97	96	95	94	93	92	91

URDU

۱	۱۱	۲۱	۳۱	۴۱	۵۱	۶۱	۷۱	۸۱	۹۱
۲	۱۲	۲۲	۳۲	۴۲	۵۲	۶۲	۷۲	۸۲	۹۲
۳	۱۳	۲۳	۳۳	۴۳	۵۳	۶۳	۷۳	۸۳	۹۳
۴	۱۴	۲۴	۳۴	۴۴	۵۴	۶۴	۷۴	۸۴	۹۴
۵	۱۵	۲۵	۳۵	۴۵	۵۵	۶۵	۷۵	۸۵	۹۵
۶	۱۶	۲۶	۳۶	۴۶	۵۶	۶۶	۷۶	۸۶	۹۶
۷	۱۷	۲۷	۳۷	۴۷	۵۷	۶۷	۷۷	۸۷	۹۷
۸	۱۸	۲۸	۳۸	۴۸	۵۸	۶۸	۷۸	۸۸	۹۸
۹	۱۹	۲۹	۳۹	۴۹	۵۹	۶۹	۷۹	۸۹	۹۹
۱۰	۲۰	۳۰	۴۰	۵۰	۶۰	۷۰	۸۰	۹۰	۱۰۰

Figure 2.5

+	1	2	3	4	5
1	2	3	4	5	6
2	3	4	5	6	7
3	4	5	6	7	8
4	5	6	7	8	9
5	6	7	8	9	10

×	1	2	3	4	5
1	1	2	3	4	5
2	2	4	6	8	10
3	3	6	9	12	15
4	4	8	12	16	20
5	5	10	15	20	25

All the grids considered so far each contain the numbers from 1 to, say, 100 in order. Addition squares and multiplication squares are also rich sources of patterns. For young children in the age-range being considered in this book, it is probably most sensible to use the squares with numbers just upto 5, say, in the columns and row headings, as in figure 2.5.

Constructing the grids themselves can involve children in spotting patterns and individuals might use these patterns to help guess which numbers will fill in different spaces.

One suggestion for an activity, from the numerous possible ones, is given below for each of the two grids.

[A] Squares within the addition square

Ask children to choose a square of numbers from the addition square, for example,

4 5 6
5 6 7
6 7 8

What can they find out about it?

Some children might list the different numbers in it and count how many times each one appears. There is a pattern to the results if the numbers are listed in order. Would the same sort of situation arise in any 3 x 3 square?

Try asking children to add up the different lines of three numbers in the square. Which different answers can be made? Are there any patterns? Why do they happen?

[B] Diagonals on the tables square

Ask children to look at the different diagonals of the table square and see what they can find out about them.

Children might notice that the numbers in the / diagonals are symmetrical. They could be asked to look at how the numbers arrived along the diagonals, so that they might see why the symmetry occurs.

There are some interesting patterns in the way the numbers along the diagonals increase. For example, in the diagonal

2
6
12
20

the numbers go up by 4, then 6, then 8. What do children think would happen if the table square were extended? Is their prediction correct?

Attention could be focused on the numbers in the main diagonal. What is special about these numbers? Which would come next?

Exploring patterns in addition and subtraction facts

It is important for children to acquire a quick working knowledge of simple number facts such as 2 + 3 = 5, 6 - 4 = 2, 2 x 4 = 8 etc. Unless one has these at one's fingertips, one is held up in making more complicated calculations. This is not the place to discuss the numerous ways in which these number bonds can be practised and learnt (for example, through the use of games), but some attention will be paid to the formation of patterns in connection with addition and subtraction facts. Multiplication will be left out here since multiplication facts have featured earlier in the activities connected with tables.

One way of producing some interesting patterns is to involve children in making the set of additions to a particular total and then in ordering them. For example, they might have 7 as a total number of cubes to aim for and try to reach this total by combining, say, red cubes and green cubes in as many ways as possible. A combination such as 3 red cubes and 4 green cubes could be recorded as 3 + 4 = 7. The record of each combination could be written on a separate slip of paper then, when the children think they have found all possible combinations, the slips could be put in order of the first number:

1 + 6 = 7
2 + 5 = 7
3 + 4 = 7 etc.

Having set the order 1, 2, 3 ... the pattern of 6, 5, 4 ... remains to be discovered. Young children, say from Year 2 or even Year 1, often seem to find this intriguing. As well as the pattern spotting, other issues are likely to arise too, such as using zero (for example, in 0 + 7 = 7) and deciding where to place this addition in the ordered set; observing that 7 can be made from 4 + 3 as well as 3 + 4 and deciding whether to count both; thinking what could come after the last entry in the list (6 + 1 = 7 if 0 has not been used and 6 + 1 is being counted as different from 1 + 6; 7 + 0 = 7 if 0 is being used). After perhaps exploring the combinations to a particular number as a group, individual children could have a go at choosing their own totals to aim for. Figure 2.6 shows 6 year old Carli's record of her ordered combinations to her own choice of 8.

Comparing how many different combinations are possible for different numbers is an activity which itself throws up some interesting patterns as can be seen from 6 year old Ian's table of results in figure 2.7.

Sometimes children make up sums which have the same total by accident. Either they themselves might decide to explore this further, or the teacher could suggest that they try to find other examples. In the activity shown here as figure 2.8, Richard, aged 5/6, was simply 'making up sums'. Having completed 17 + 5 = 22, he then went on to 16 + 7 = 23 and 15 + 8 = 23. He commented about both these last two answers being the same, thought about why that might be and decided to try making another sum by adding one less than the 15 and one more than the 8. He was delighted that this too gave 23 as he had hoped and went on to produce two more sums similarly. Having completed 12 + 11 he realized that the next sum would be 11 + 12 and said he would leave that because it was 'the same'. He decided to try to make 24 instead, which he did from 16 + 8, then transformed that addition to 15 + 9 to produce the same answer again.

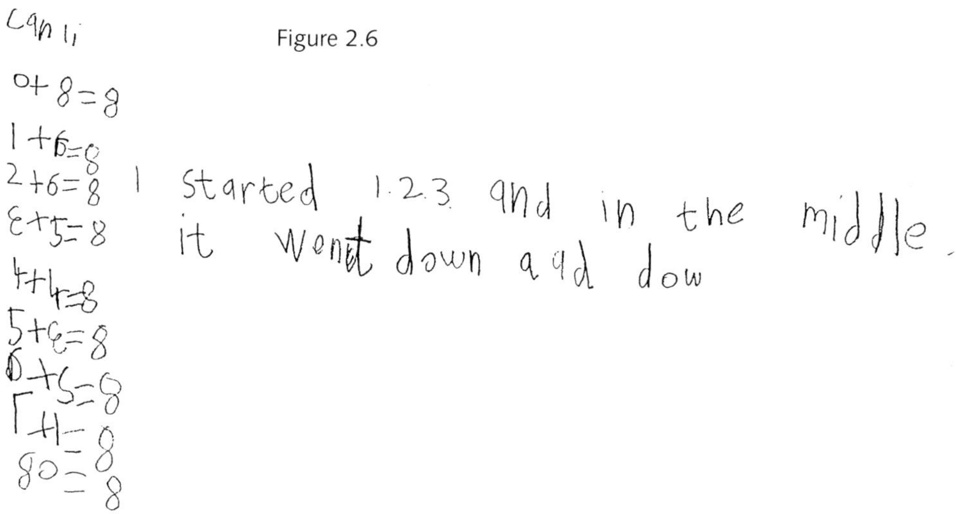

Figure 2.6

Figure 2.7

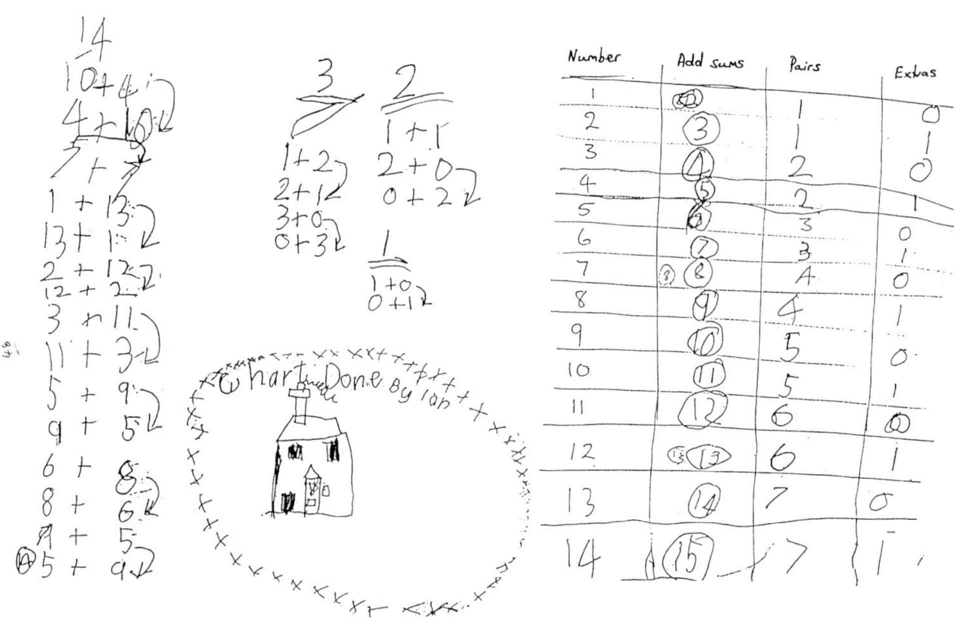

Figure 2.8

Subtraction patterns can also be built up and ordered, for example as in

$$10 - 1 = 9$$
$$11 - 2 = 9$$
$$12 - 3 = 9$$
$$13 - 4 = 9 \text{ etc.}$$

This list of subtractions can, of course, be extended indefinitely and some awareness of the fact that the list could go on and on for ever has the potential to give young children one of their first insights into the idea that some processes are unlimited.

Looking at the answers formed from doubling small numbers can prove interesting. Having worked out a number of additions such as 2 + 2 = 4, 5 + 5 = 10, children could pool their answers and see where they occur on a number ladder. Some children see the results as a 'do one, miss one' type pattern. Predictions can be encouraged as to how the pattern will continue and children might try to find additions to fit the predictions. Such a situation arose through a 5 year old's own choice of numbers of biscuits to put together on a series of pairs of plates: see the 'Plates of biscuits' case study in Bird (1991), chapter 7. Giving a free hand to children to make up their own additions, whether embedded in a context or not and with or without materials, often results in the production of answers in some sort of pattern. Children may well be unaware of such patterns at first, but the teacher could draw attention to them, perhaps with the use of number ladders as just mentioned.

Another possible activity is to find the total number of ways of splitting a number into additions. For example, 5 not only equals 0 + 5, 1 + 4 and 2 + 3, it also equals 1 + 1 + 1 + 1 + 1, 3 + 1 + 1, 2 + 2 + 1 etc. A convenient way for children to build up such combinations is for them to use Cuisenaire rods or Colour Factor. The activity could begin by asking children how many 'trains' they can make which are the same length as a particular rod, say the pink (4) rod in Cuisenaire. Decisions would have to be made as to whether, say, a green rod followed by a white rod is to be counted as the same as a white rod followed by a green rod. Children could decide on the rule themselves. Figure 2.9 shows the complete set of arrangements (or 'partitions' as they are often termed) equivalent to the green rod (3), where a changed position of the same set of rods counts separately. Can children be certain they have finished finding all combinations when they think they have done so? The arrangements could subsequently be translated into numbers and additions hence built up.

Figure 2.9

The complete set of partitions for different rods (and hence the complete set of additions for different numbers), could be compared. Some interesting patterns arise whichever rule the children decide on for allowing or not allowing a different arrangement of the same rods. It is also interesting to explore the number of rows in a partition which contain 1 rod, 2 rods, 3 rods etc. For example, for the pink (4) rod and with different arrangements of the same rods counting as different, there is 1 row with 1 rod; 3 rows with 2 rods; 3 rows with 3 rods; 1 row with 4 rods, hence a pattern of 1, 3, 3, 1. What happens with other rods? And are there any connections between the results for different partitions? 2

Patterns concerned with tens and units

Try asking children to work out the answers to sets of additions such as

6 + 3 =	5 + 10 =
16 + 3 =	15 + 10 =
26 + 3 =	25 + 10 =
36 + 3 =	35 + 10 =
46 + 3 = etc.	45 + 10 = etc.

An example like the second one is given to illustrate part of the requirements of level 3 of Attainment Target 3 in the National Curriculum document. One concern, however, is that children might carry out these additions and notice a pattern in the answers but never reach the 'so what?' stage. They really need to be encouraged to think and discuss why the patterns occur. Another way to encourage more active thinking would be to invite children to make up their own examples of similar patterns once they have tried the teacher's. This should help them to focus on the structure behind such examples.

The National Curriculum document also gives the following as an example of using patterns in number when doing mental calculations:

Find 27 + 31 by: $27 + 31 = 20 + 7 + 30 + 1$

$= 50 + 8$

$= 58$

It is perfectly possible to involve children in carrying out lots of additions by splitting up and re-grouping numbers in the way illustrated. However, such calculations could again be carried out blindly. It seems vital that the whole process is discussed and the significance established. Again, children could be encouraged to make up their own examples and talk about them. See Jonathan's (6/7) page of his own choice of calculations in figure 2.10. Note that he wrote the second line of each of the three sums before inserting the answer in the first line.

Figure 2.10

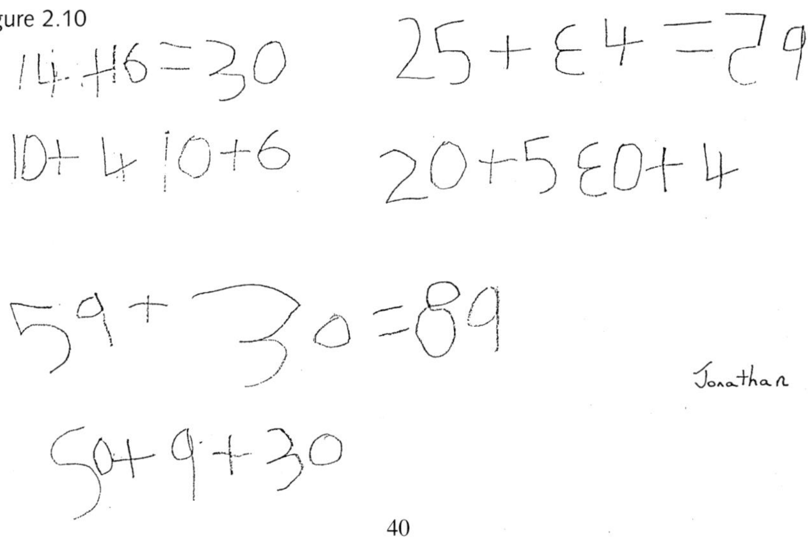

Awareness of underlying structure is likely to arise incidentally when children are working on number explorations in any case. For example, see the comments in the second case study at the end of this chapter about Warren discovering that 10 + 11 gave the same answer as 20 + 1 and then reasoning why this was the case. This links with the comments about Richard's work on p.It seems sensible for the teacher to be on the look out for such instances and to discuss them, perhaps with other children too, as they arise. Again, children could be asked to make up and explain further examples.

Some patterns concerned with tens and units may be hard for children actually to explain at this stage but may, nevertheless, prove fascinating to explore. For example, children capable of tens and units subtraction with exchange may well become intrigued by the following activity:

> Choose a two digit number (for example, 26). Reverse it (62). Find the difference between these two numbers (36). Repeat for other choices of two-digit numbers.

When one group of 7/8 year olds worked on this they became involved in such things as the following:

- Discussing how they carried out the subtractions, both mentally and on paper;
- Discussing how they recorded their subtractions on paper;
- Comparing the answers;
- Noticing that some answers were the same;
- Ordering the answers, noticing that most went 'up in 9s'; then realizing there was a gap in the sequence; finding an answer to fill the gap;
- Reinterpreting adding 9s as 'timesing by 9';
- Making a generalization about which numbers would give 0 as an answer;
- Extending the investigation to 3 digit numbers.

See figures 2.11 and 2.12 for snippets of two of the children's work. For more details, see also Bird (1986), chapter 1.

Figure 2.11

Figure 2.12

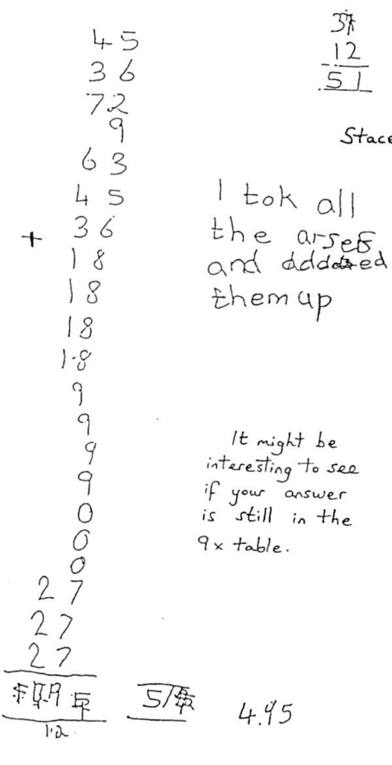

THE NATIONAL CURRICULUM FOR KEY STAGE 1 MATHEMATICS

The activities discussed in this chapter concentrate mainly on Number: 3b from the Programme of Study, namely:

> 'Explore and record patterns in addition and subtraction, and then patterns of multiples, explaining their patterns and using them to make predictions; progress to exploring further patterns involving multiplication and division, including those within a hundred-square of multiplication facts.'

Alongside this major area, there is also scope for a lot of emphasis on other items from the Number section of the Programme of Study. In particular, there will be opportunities for pupils to:

> 'develop flexible methods of working with number, orally and mentally' (1a);
>
> 'use calculators both as a means to explore number and as a tool for calculating with realistic data' (1d);
>
> 'record in a variety of ways, including ways that relate to their mental work' (1e);
>
> 'count orally up to 10 and beyond, knowing the number names; ... count in steps of different sizes; recognise sequences ...' (from 2a);
>
> 'read, write and order numbers, initially to 10, progressing up to 1000, developing an understanding that the position of a digit signifies its value ...' (from 2b);
>
> 'use repeating patterns to develop ideas of regularity and sequencing' (3a);
>
> 'know addition and subtraction facts to 20, and develop a range of mental methods for finding, from known facts, those that they cannot recall; learn multiplication and division facts relating to the 2s, 5s, 10s, and use these to learn other facts, eg double multiples of 2 to produce multiples of 4, and to develop mental mathods for finding new results' (3c);
>
> 'develop a variety of methods for adding and subtracting ...' (from 3d);
>
> 'use a basic calculator, reading the display' (3e);
>
> 'undertand the operations of addition, subtraction ...' (from 4a);
>
> 'understand the operations of multiplication, and division ...' (from 4b);
>
> 'choose a suitable method of computation, using apparatus where appropriate, or a calculator where the numbers include several digits' (4c).

Furthermore, there is also scope for a lot of emphasis on the following items from the Using and Applying Mathematics section of the Programme of Study:

'use and apply mathematics ... within mathematics itself' (from 1a);

'explain their thinking to support the development of their reasoning' (1b);

'organise and check their work' (2d);

'understand the language of number ...' (from 3a);

'relate numerals and other mathematical symbols, eg '+', '=', to a range of situations' (3b);

'discuss their work, responding to and asking mathematical questions' (3c);

'recognise simple patterns and relationships and make related predictions about them' (4a);

'ask questions including "What would happen if?" and "Why?"' (4b);

'understand general statements and investigate whether particular cases match them' (4c).

Case study: Continuous addition patterns

I asked a group of 'middle ability' top infants each to choose a number between 1 and 10 and enter it in a calculator. I imposed the starting limit of 10 partly so that the numbers subsequently produced would be ones with which the children would be familiar at least at first, and partly to give the children the opportunity of choosing to start beyond 10 later on in the activity, if appropriate.

Neil chose 9, Michelle 2, Marie 4 and Mark 100 (!) but then 10 when reminded of the limits. Then I asked them to add 5 to the number, then add 5 again, then again and so on and to keep looking at the numbers they obtained to see if they noticed anything. I also suggested that they wrote down the numbers because that would help them compare them.

The children set about the task by themselves. When I checked on them after a little while, although each member of the group had produced a chain of several numbers, nobody had noticed anything about them. I realized that this was probably because they had been writing in the '+5' as well, with the result that the answers were not side by side and hence were rather difficult to compare. It was interesting to note in passing that Marie had written her sums correctly symbolically, (see figure 2.13) whereas the others had written such things as '10+5=15+5=20' (see figure 2.14 for example).

Figure 2.13

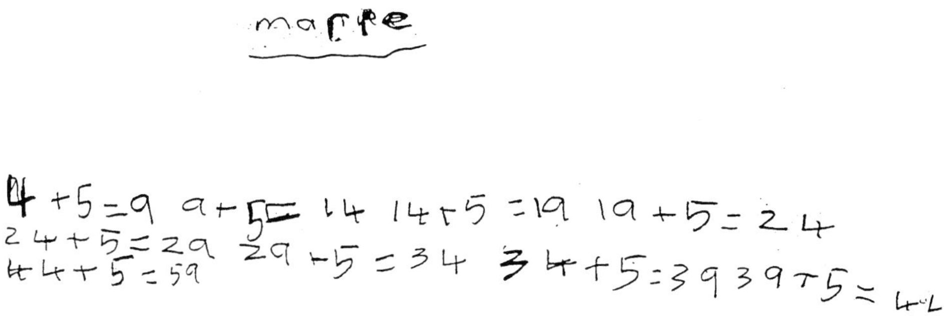

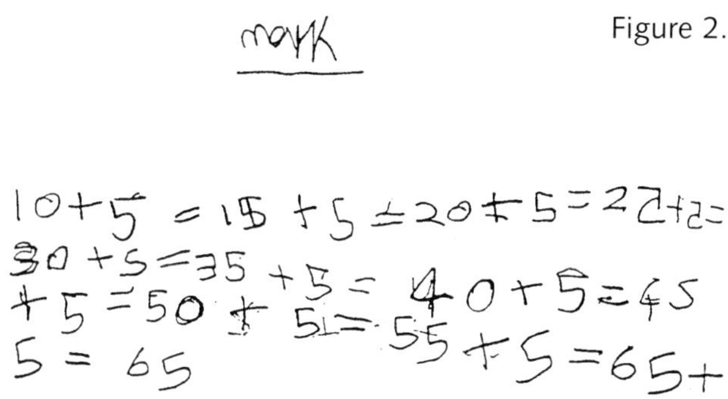

Figure 2.14

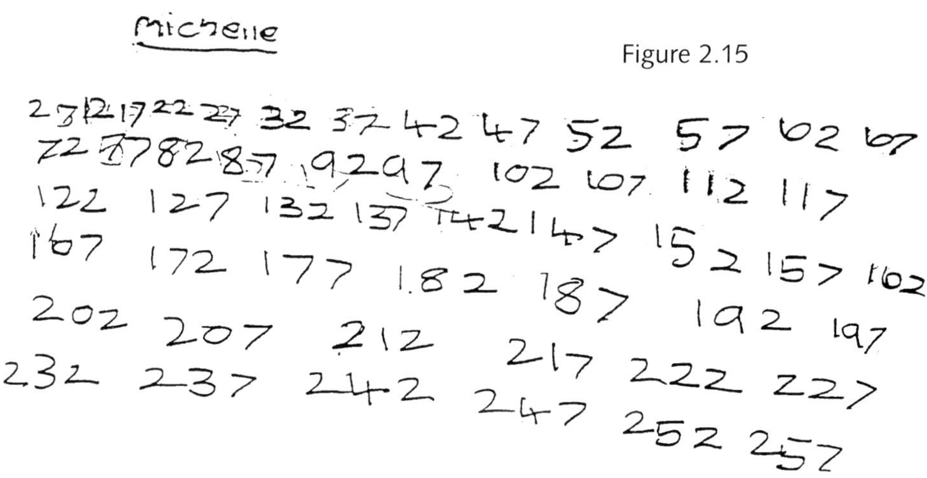

Figure 2.15

Figure 2.16

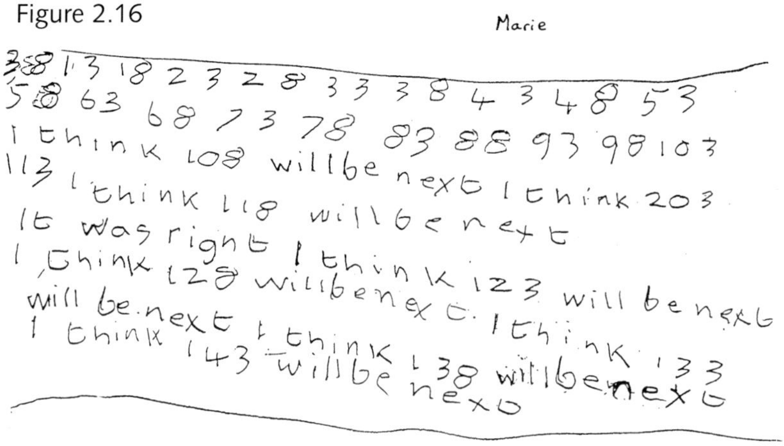

Figure 2.17

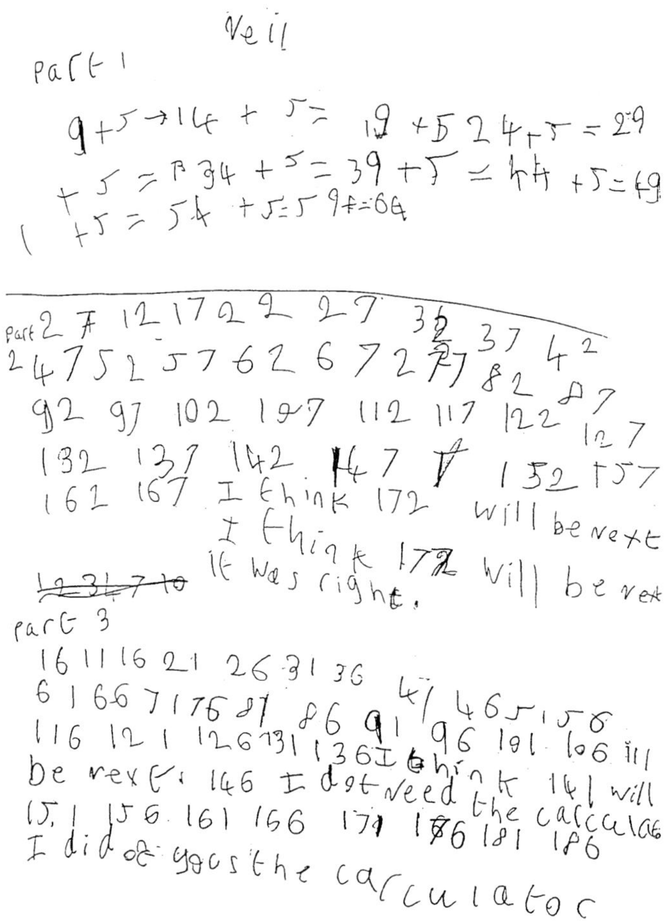

The latter is, of course, a common occurrence and was perfectly sensible as a record of what the children were doing. I made a mental note that we might compare the symbolisms at some point to see if the children could find any problems with the non-standard form.

Michelle had discovered that the 'equals' key could be used to keep adding on 5. I suggested that the rest tried this out too and that, this time, they wrote down just the answers arrived at so that they could see where they were on their papers more easily. Michelle started with her original number again (2), but Neil, Mark and Marie changed theirs to 2, 9 and 3 respectively.

The children set about the task and continued by themselves. The next time that I asked them if they had noticed anything they had lots to offer. Each appeared to be aware of the pattern in the units which they expressed as 'It goes 3,8,3,8,3,8...' etc. Michelle had also noticed a pattern in the tens. Pointing to the appropriate figures she said '1,1,2,2,3,3,4,4' (see figure 2.15). I wished afterwards that I had asked her to continue to see how she coped with reading off the tens in numbers such as 102, 137 etc.

The children were quite excited by the patterns. At one point, looking at a number on his calculator, Mark exclaimed 'I was right' suggesting that he had predicted ahead. I encouraged the others to think ahead too. To us, this might seem a really simple procedure, but for these young children it was quite challenging and sometimes it took quite a while for them to work out what the answer would be. Figure 2.16 shows Marie's work at this stage and it is interesting to see how she predicted 203 after 108 but, having found the result was 113, correctly predicted 118 for the next one.

The children tried starting with other numbers as well and were interested to find the same sort of thing happening. The whole of Neil's work is shown in figure 2.17. His written remarks in what he called 'part 3' are worthy of particular note. He was delighted with the idea of continuing the number pattern by himself.

Case study: Adding numbers from columns of a 1 to 100 square

I gave each of a group of 6/7 year olds a piece of paper with a 1 to 100 square printed on the top half of it. The children were familiar with these grids and said that they had used them before. I said that they would be doing something different with them this time.

Giving out a green and a red pencil to each child, I asked them to colour in one column of numbers green and another column of numbers red. I showed them what I meant by a column and said that they could each choose which they liked.

Once the colouring had been completed, I asked the children each to pick a number from the green column and a number from the red column and to add them together, using a calculator if they wanted to do so. I suggested that they make a note of the answers. In fact they all recorded the actual sums too. I said that, after they had finished their first addition, they could go on to do lots of other examples too, the same way. They worked at the task without any assistance.

Figure 2.18

1	2	3	4	5	6	7	8	9	10
11	12	13	14	15	16	17	18	19	20
21	22	23	24	25	26	27	28	29	30
31	32	33	34	35	36	37	38	39	40
41	42	43	44	45	46	47	48	49	50
51	52	53	54	55	56	57	58	59	60
61	62	63	64	65	66	67	68	69	70
71	72	73	74	75	76	77	78	79	80
81	82	83	84	85	86	87	88	89	90
91	92	93	94	95	96	97	98	99	100

21 + 37 = 58 thay All End in 8tse

91 + 97 = 188

77 + 71 = 148

1 + 7 = 8

11 + 17 = 28

27 + 21 = 48

81 + 7 88

7 + 91 = 98

Figure 2.19

Pf

1	2	3	4	5	6	7	8	9	10
11	12	13	14	15	16	17	18	19	20
21	22	23	24	25	26	27	28	29	30
31	32	33	34	35	36	37	38	39	40
41	42	43	44	45	46	47	48	49	50
51	52	53	54	55	56	57	58	59	60
61	62	63	64	65	66	67	68	69	70
71	72	73	74	75	76	77	78	79	80
81	82	83	84	85	86	87	88	89	90
91	92	93	94	95	96	97	98	99	100

14 + 6 = 20
4 + 16 = 20
24 + 26 = 50
34 + 36 = 70
44 + 46 = 90
54 + 56 = 110

Oh mine
they all end
Wtth 0

After a while I checked to see what was happening. The children were eager to tell me what they had noticed. Claire, who had been taking numbers from the columns headed by 2 and 4, had found that all her answers 'have got 6 at the end'; Paul, working from the columns headed by 4 and 6, had found that all his answers 'end in 0'; Warren, who had chosen the columns headed by 1 and 10, had obtained answers which 'end in 1'; and Rebecca, working within columns headed by 1 and 7, had obtained answers which 'end in 8'. Nobody commented on any connections between the column headings and the results.Warren also pointed out that two of his sums, namely 10+11 and 20+1, both gave 21 as the answer. He seemed puzzled by this but then exclaimed 'Oh! 20 is 10 and 10.' Further discussion with him revealed that he could see how the

10+11 was10+10+1 and the 20+1 was10+10+1.

I asked if anybody else had two answers the same. Paul said that he had and offered 14+6=20 and 4+16=20. When asked why he thought these gave the same answer he spotted that the '1 is just in a different place.' Further probing revealed that he was aware that this '1' was really a ten and that he could perceive the first expression split up as 10+4+6 and the second as 4+10+6.

Two pieces of the children's work are shown in figures 2.18 and 2.19. It is interesting to note that, after his first crossover of 14 with 6 and 4 with 16, Paul has started to go down both columns on the same horizontal level. It would have been interesting to have seen if he noticed a pattern in his answers. He was the only child of whom I was aware who put consistent structuring into his choice of numbers. This, of course, was not required by the opening idea.

Notes

1. I am grateful to a former student, Michelle Worsley, for suggesting this idea. Her work with 6/7 year olds showed that whereas some children seemed to choose particular lines of numbers because they could see a pattern in the numbers, other children chose lines without thinking about the numbers first. In this latter case, some of the children then seemed to think quite hard about the numbers picked out by the line, before commenting on them.

2. See the section entitled 'Partitions' in chapter 9 of the Association of Teachers of Mathematics; Notes on mathematics in primary schools; Cambridge University Press; 1967; pp. 201-4. There are a number of other interesting references to the use of Cuisenaire Rods in the text.

Chapter Three: Properties

As children learn more and more about number, so they will find out that there are particular sorts of numbers which behave in special wasys. These sorts of numbers include square numbers, triangular numbers, cube numbers and prime numbers etc. but, for children in the age-range under consideration in this book, the main concentration is likely to be simply on the differences between odd and even numbers.

Becoming familiar with odds and evens

There are many ways through which children might first become acquainted with odd and even numbers. Frequently used ways include having attention drawn to the numbers on houses on opposite sides of a street and looking at the numbers on the right and left hand pages of a book. These observations can themselves incorporate some elements of enquiry as can be seen from the start of the first case study at the end of this chapter. Perhaps not so frequently used is the way in which sets of odd and even numbers can emerge as a result of exploratory number activities and these sets can then be examined in their own right. For instance, some children arrived at even numbers in the plates of biscuits example referred to on p.They could be invited to see where the answers occur on a number ladder, attention could be drawn to the pattern, and more numbers found which fit the pattern and more which do not. The children could be told that the numbers in the pattern are often referred to as 'even' numbers and those not in the pattern as 'odd' numbers.

Here are two other activities in which a distinction between odd and even numbers is likely to arise in the course of exploration:

[A] Coloured strips

Give children different length strips of squares, asking them to colour the squares alternately, using two different colours.

There is potential here for children to focus on which length strips begin and end in the same colours (for example, a 7-square strip coloured red, green, red, green etc. would begin and end on red) and which length strips begin and end on different colours. Classifying these different types of strips, sorts the numbers of squares into odds and evens.

Lots of other interesting questions/issues can arise incidentally through working on this activity. As examples:

(1) After a child has completed a strip which, say, starts and ends in red, a good question to ask would be how the strip would end if it starts in green. Although the answer to this is obvious to us, this may be far from the case for young children.

(2) There may well be a debate about how to colour and classify a strip composed of just one square. Ilona (4/5 years) exclaimed 'You can't do a one-one pattern on a one-square!' but Jemma (4/5 years) said that she could 'just do one colour' and Ilona did so, colouring it green. Later, when sorting the strips into piles. Matthew (4/5 years) held up Ilona's single green square and queried 'Is that a "both green"?' Ilona said they could put it in the 'both green' pile and Jemma was happy to agree. Reinforcement for this being sensible came later when the children realized that it fitted in with the 3, 5, 7 ... pattern established for strips which start and end with the same colour. 1

(3) Given a pile of different length strips, children might set themselves the task of completing one of each length and hence search for different strips in order, or try to find strips which fit gaps between the ones already completed.

(4) There are opportunities to make and test predictions such as thinking ahead how a particular strip will behave, based on knowledge of what has happened with others.

There are possibilities for extensions too. Using more than two colours is likely to lead to a focus on sets of numbers other than odds and evens. For example, strips within which a sequence of three colours starts and ends exactly are of length 3, 6, 9, 12 etc. Children may well suggest using different numbers of colours of their own accord. For instance, having been using red and green to colour his strips, Joseph (4/5 years) asked if he could now use yellow as well so that he could have 'all the traffic lights'!

[B] Making two equal piles

Ask children to take a pile of cubes (or buttons, counters etc.) and try to split it into two piles with the same number of cubes in each. For which numbers of cubes does this work? And for which does it not?

Sometimes, instead of sharing the cubes into two piles, some children split the cubes into sets of two. This in itself will, of course, lead to a distinction between odd and even numbers, so from the point of view of the end result of the activity, it does not really matter how the task is interpreted. However, teachers might well want to draw attention to the distinction between the language: splitting into two sets (including two equal sets as in this example) is not the same as splitting into sets of two.

Having found several numbers of cubes which can be split into two equal piles, and, perhaps, having seen where the numbers occur on a number ladder, children could be asked to predict what will happen with other numbers. Figure 3.1 shows how Joanne (6/7 years) recorded the activity with numbers up to 10. She wrote the tick by 6 and the cross by 9 on the left hand side of the ladder to indicate that these were guesses at first, based on some of the other results. Figure 3.2 shows Brett's (6/7 years) extension of the activity beyond 10. He predicted all the over 10 results, then checked those for 16, 17, 18 and 19. Readers might enjoy trying to work out what he has written!

Having experimented with small numbers of cubes, children might be invited to choose a really large number and asked to decide whether these could be split into two piles exactly. Could they tell whether it would work without actually doing it? Similar questions could, of course, be asked within activities such as the 'Coloured strips' one above.

There is potential for the exploration to be extended into splitting sets of cubes into three equal piles, four equal piles etc.

Figure 3.1

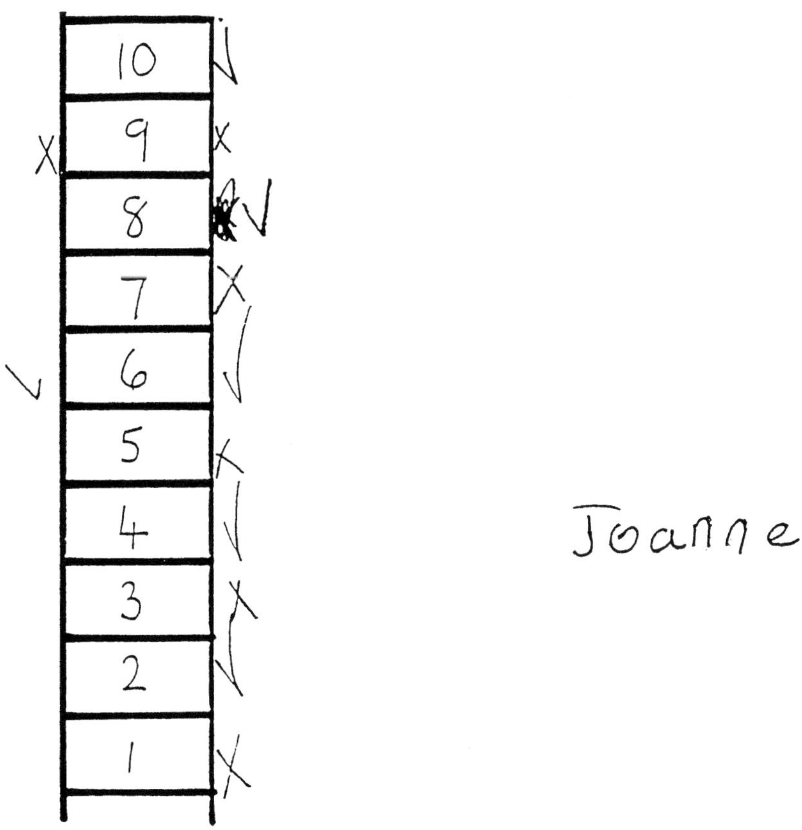

Figure 3.2

Using the idea of odds and evens

Once children are aware of 'odds' and 'evens' as two different sorts of numbers, opportunities could be created for them to use the concepts in further activities. This should help with their familiarization of the terms as well as providing scope for further awareness of properties. Some suggestions follow of activities which can give rise to some interesting explorations.

[A] A grid activity

Children could be given grids consisting of, say, four by four squares as in figure 3.3, and a particular number of counters, say twelve. They could then be asked to try to find a way of placing the counters in the squares so that each row and column has an even number of counters in it.

Figure 3.3

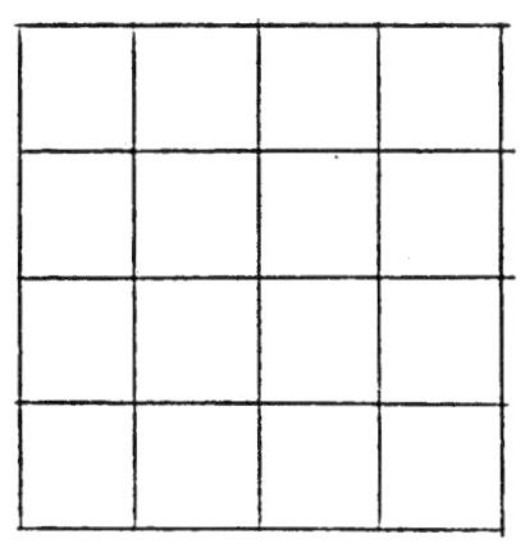

Sometimes children solve the puzzle in one direction, for example vertically as in figure 3.4, but not in the other direction. They can then be encouraged to see if they can move just a few of the counters to make the pattern work both ways.

Figure 3.4

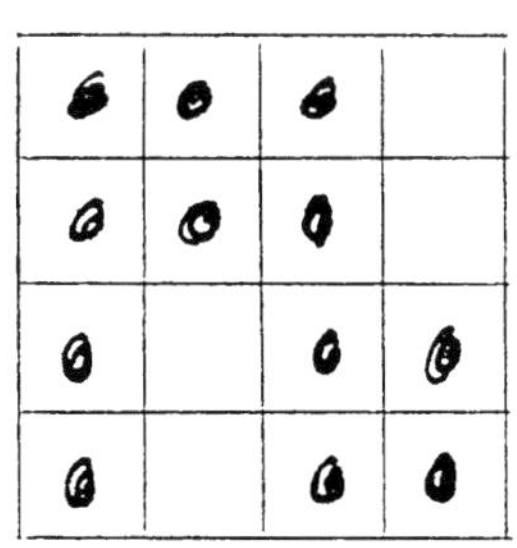

Figure 3.5

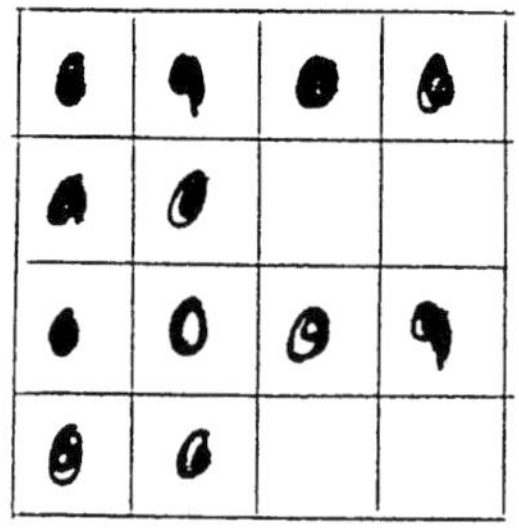

Questions are begged such as 'Is this pattern the same as this?', for example, compare figures 3.5 and 3.6. Children can be involved in deciding on their own rules to determine which patterns will be called the 'same' and which 'different'. For a particular rule, children could try to exhaust all the possible arrangements. How many are there? Can they be certain they have found them all?

Figure 3.6

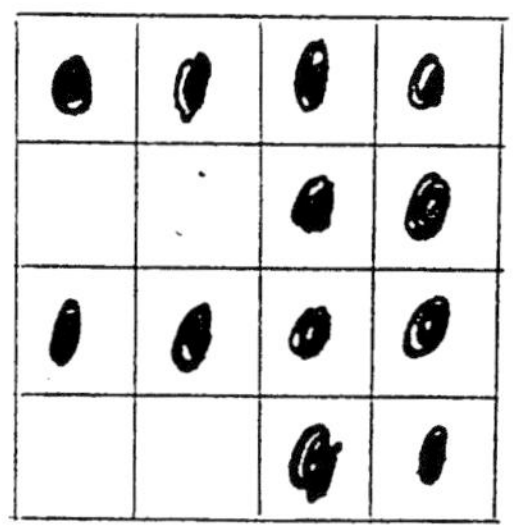

A possible extension is for children to choose their own size grid; or their own number of counters; or which to aim for: odd or even; or any combination of these variations! There is a great deal of scope for exploration here.

Sometimes children choose combinations of fixed conditions for which there turn out to be no solutions. For example, David (5 years) chose to use ten counters on a four by four grid and to try to make the number of counters in each row even. He spent a long time trying to obtain a solution but found each time that he was left with an odd number of counters in some lines. Such experience can start to help provide an early awareness of 'impossibility'. As mentioned in chapter 1, it is important that children are encouraged to realize that to show something is impossible is just as important as finding a solution, otherwise they may become dispirited and want to give up. To continue the example above, David went on to try a smaller number of counters (six) on the same size grid and to aim for an odd number in each line. His results are shown in figure 3.7. One of these is not correct, but the achievement as a whole is quite remarkable for a child not yet 6.

Figure 3.7

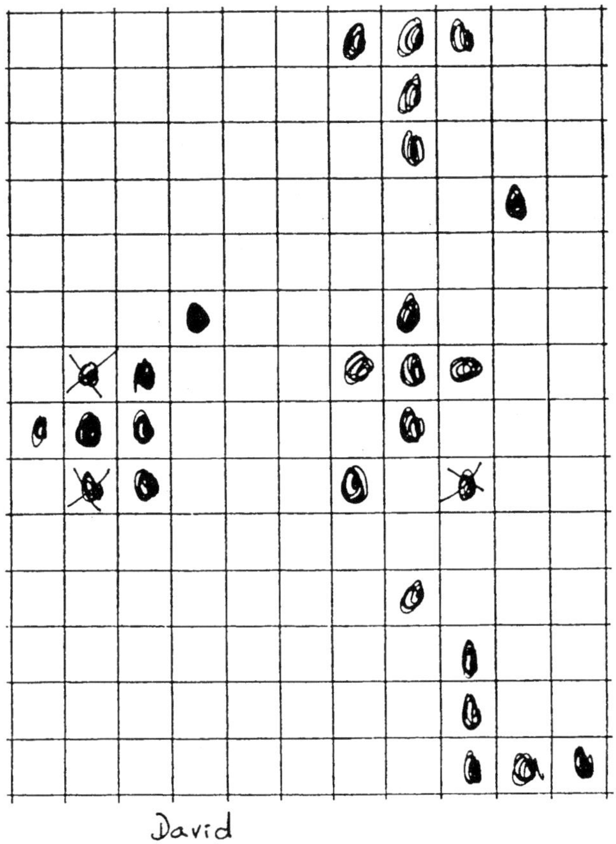

[B] Different numbers of columns

The idea has already been mentioned (see chapter 2, p.) of colouring, say, every other number, or every third number etc. on number grids set out with different numbers of columns. This activity could be begun with children explicitly looking for even numbers or odd numbers in the grids and comparing the results of different size grids.

Points made about the activity in chapter 2 apply equally well here and so will not be repeated. However, a case study of children working on the odd/even version is included at the end of this chapter because of the further insights this gives into facets of young children's learning.

Patterns of odd and even numbers can also be explored on other arrangements of numbers. For example, see figure 3.8 for a copy of 6 year old Michelle's colouring of odds and evens on a given spiral of numbers. She saw that this gave a pattern of

yellow
blue
yellow
blue etc.

also: yellow blue yellow blue too.

She went on to make her own choice of arrangement within the spiral as can be seen in figure 3.9.

Figure 3.8

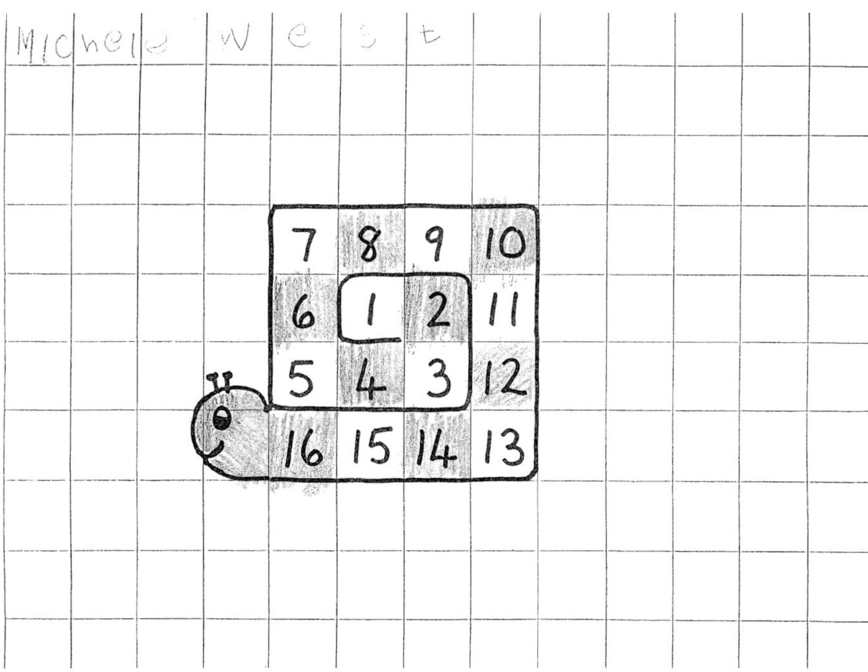

Figure 3.9

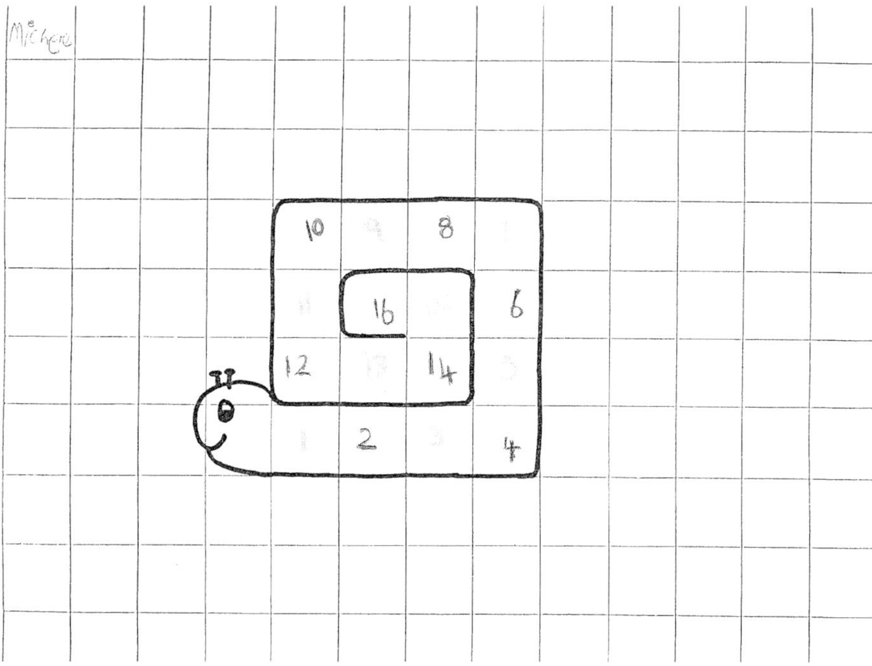

[C] Dominoes

Numerous activities can be carried out with sets of dominoes other than the standard matching or threes-and-fives games and some of these can require explicit attention to odd and even numbers. A simple example is to play a matching game in which any odd number can be placed by an odd number and any even by any even. This is likely to throw up the issue of what a 'blank' can be counted as.

Another activity is to sort out all the dominoes containing even numbers into one pile and all those containing odd numbers into another pile. This begs the question: what about dominoes with odd and even numbers on them? As a follow-up to this activity, it is interesting to see how many dominoes there are in each set and explain why the totals are different: in particular, why is there such a small number of dominoes containing just odd numbers?

Figure 3.10 shows how Robert (8 years) arranged the dominoes in the three sets. To make a structured arrangement was completely his own idea. Talking with him after he had completed the sets revealed that he had started with the all-even dominoes, arranging them according to the total numbers of spots on each. Not only did he then order these totals starting from the smallest, 0, and increasing by two each time to 12, he also arranged the dominoes within each total so that the right hand sides increased by two each time. See the middle of figure 3.10 for this complex structuring. He then went on to arrange the other two sets in similar ways.

Figure 3.10

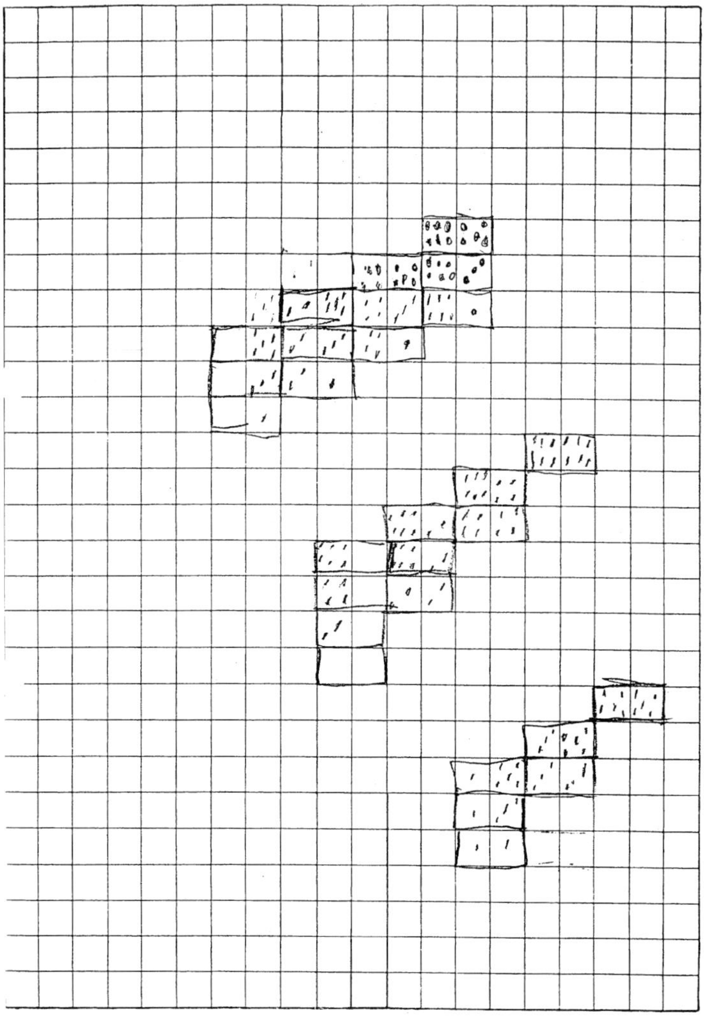

[D] Cross game

A game can be played using the board shown in figure 3.11 together with, say, twelve little pieces of card, six of which have 'odd' written on them and six 'even'. Two players each start with a counter in the middle square. The cards are placed face downwards and the children take it in turns to turn one over. If the card says 'odd', then the player has to move an odd number of spaces; if 'even', then an even number of spaces. The aim is to land on the shaded squares and collect the number of points shown. The game ends when all the cards have been turned over and the winner is the child who has collected the greatest number of points.

Figure 3.11

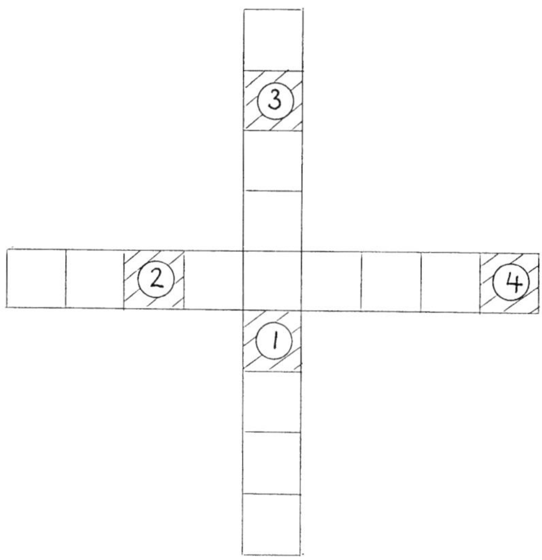

Playing the game involves children in continuously having to think which of the numbers up to 7 (the maximum number of spaces from one shaded square to another) are odd and which are even. As the game proceeds, some children actually start to remember how many spaces there are between particular pairs of numbers and whether these are odd or even. Some children also notice things about their particular set of scores. For example, Jonathan (8 years) commented on not having 1 as a score at all in his list. He said that this was because he was always aiming for the highest possible number. When asked if he would never score a 1, then, he was able to reason that he would in fact do so if he were on '3' already and picked up a card which said 'even', since to go to 2 or 4 required an odd number of jumps. On playing the game again, he did indeed need to score 1 in the manner he had anticipated and he drew my attention to this.

Having played on the given grid a few times, children could be invited to design their own boards and then to try them out.

[E] Adding odds and evens

Points such as the fact that two odd numbers added together always give an even number, can, of course, be discovered by children after experimenting with different numbers of their choice. See, for example, figure 3.12. Natalie's (aged 7/8) work is taken from a case study in Bird (1986), p.29. Possible extensions to this sort of activity include:

(1) Ask children to try to think why an odd number plus an odd number is always an even number, etc.

(2) Children could add pairs of consecutive odd numbers (or even numbers) and see what they can find out about the answers.

(3) Operations other than addition can be tried.

Figure 3.12

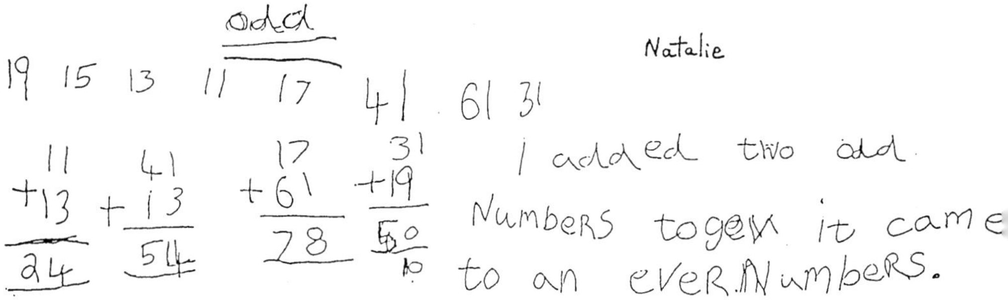

Multiples of 2, 5 and 10

Being an even number is, of course, synonymous with being a 'multiple of 2' or being in the '2 x table'. Children can learn to recognize which numbers are multiples of 2 simply by looking at the units digit. Similarly, multiples of 5 and 10 can be recognized from the units.

Explorations with tables patterns have already been discussed in chapter 2. When children have found, say, the pattern in the units for the 5 x table, they could be asked if other particular numbers (as examples, 63, 46, 95) would lie in the 5 x table if it were extended. Children seem to enjoy making up numbers for each other to say whether they are in the 5 x table or not. The same is true of the 2 x table and 10 x table too.

The following are two suggestions for further work on multiples of 2, 5 and 10:

[A] A collection game

This is a game in which one child calls out numbers written on pieces of card and these are claimed, as appropriate, by a child collecting numbers in the 2 x table, or a child collecting numbers in the 5 x table, or a child collecting numbers in the 10 x table. Every time a child claims a number in her table, she gains a point, the object being to try to gain the most points within a time limit.

It is interesting to see what happens when a number like 60 is called out. If the children notice the problem, what do they decide to do about it? Questions are begged such as will the 2 x and 5 x table children always have a number to claim when the 10 x table child does? Why is that the case? Who is likely to win the game? Could the game be made fairer for the 10 x table child?

[B] Assigning numbers to the 2 x and 5 x tables

An activity similar to the one above, but which is not a game, is as follows:

A group of children are given little pieces of paper with a number from 1 to 30 on each, and two hoops, perhaps of different colours. They are then asked to put any numbers in the 2 x table in one hoop, and any numbers in the 5 x table in the other hoop. The children have to decide what to do with numbers such as 13 which have no 'home' and numbers such as 10 which have more than one.

20 was the first number in the two homes category to be picked up by a group of 7 year olds with whom I was working. Warren, who had picked the number up, sat looking puzzled, but Tuesday (a little girl) moved the hoops so that they were touching and balanced the square of paper with the 20 on it on top of where the two rims met! I said that this was a good idea, but asked what would happen if we found more numbers like 20, meaning that there might not be enough room to balance other numbers in the same way. Without saying anything, Paul leant forward and moved one of the hoops slightly over the other one and put the number 20 in the newly created space. Warren exclaimed, 'Oh! We've done that before!' and the others also recalled some earlier work in another class which appeared to have been focused on the intersection of sets. The children who later picked up 10 and 30 put them with the 20 without any bother.

Children can be asked to see what is special about the numbers in the middle space. To make the activity more open-ended and to provide opportunities for the setting of challenges, children can then be encouraged to choose some of their own numbers above 30 and work out where they should go. Warren's choice of numbers are shown circled on his record of his work in figure 3.13. He set himself the challenge of going up to 200 in the middle region and achieved this aim.

Sometimes, when choosing their own numbers to go in the spaces, children repeat numbers already there. Instead of just ignoring them or crossing them out, the children can be invited to change them to numbers greater than 30 which are in the correct region. Hence, for example, Paul changed an extra 25 in the 5 x table section to a 35. Tuesday, who had placed an extra 30 incorrectly in the 'just 2 x table' section, thoughtfully changed it to 38.

As a further extension to the activity, children can be invited to make up their own examples, using their own choices of tables for the hoops. See figure 3.14 for Scott's work which shows that he chose the 10 x table and the 15 x table to go in the hoops!

Further activities can be centred on the following questions:

(1) Are there any rules for deciding which numbers go in the middle section?

(2) Can you find some tables which leave a section of the diagram blank?

(3) The 12 x table is in the middle section of a diagram. Which tables could be in the outer sections? Any alternatives?

These might seem quite demanding at first, but may well be appropriate for some able 7 and 8 year olds who become absorbed in deciding on their own choices of tables.

Figure 3.13

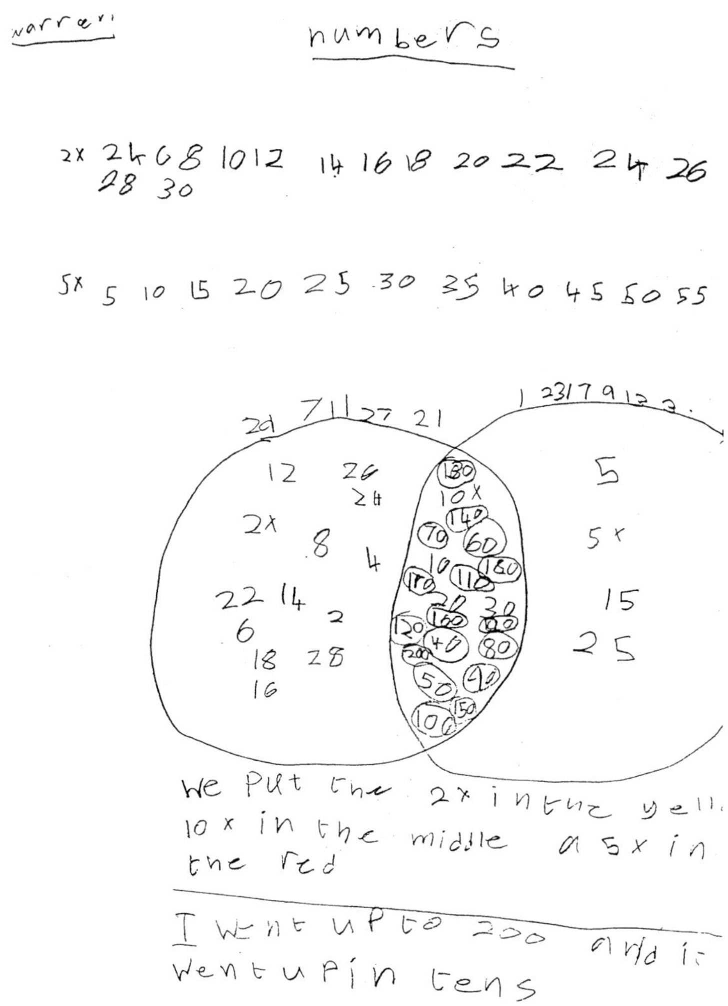

Figure 3.14

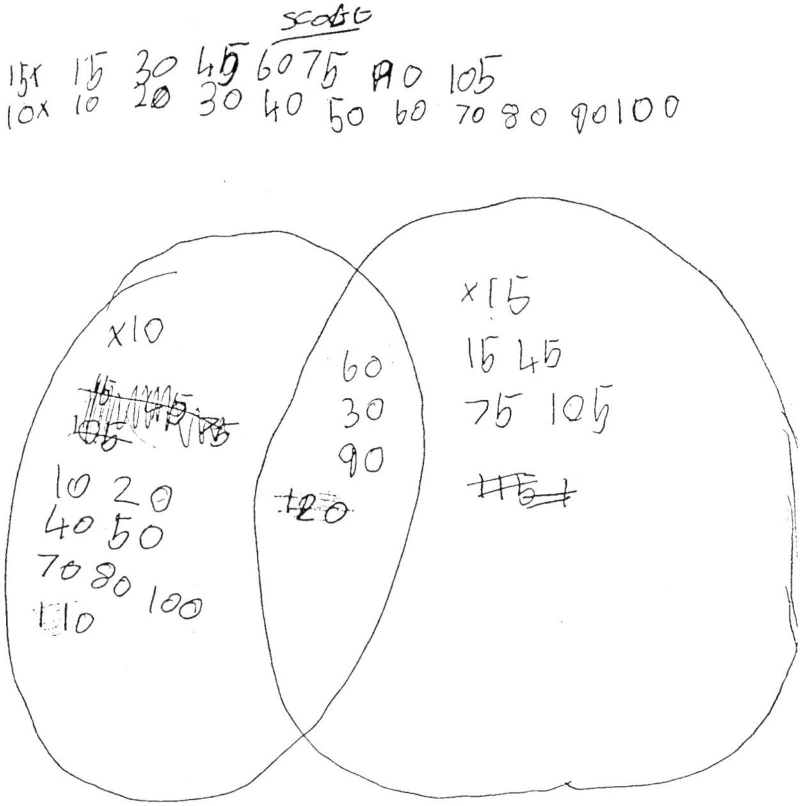

Commutativity of addition

Not only do different sorts of numbers have properties, the arithmetical operations have certain properties too.

One of the basic properties of addition which it seems appropriate for young children to encounter is that it is commutative: it does not matter whether one works out, say, 3 add 4 or 4 add 3, the result will be the same. For young children, this is of particular importance in situations such as being given 1 object and then being required to add 9 other objects to it: one can simply start with the 9 and add 1 instead of having to start with the 1 and add 9. This might seem trivial to us because we know immediately what 1 + 9 is in any case, but this is not the case when one is beginning to learn how to add.

Cuisenaire and Colour Factor

Working with materials such as Cuisenaire rods or Colour Factor may give children a good perceptual grounding of laws like commutativity for it can be readily seen that, say, a 'train' consisting of a green rod and a pink rod is the same length as a train consisting of a pink rod and a green rod. Teachers could draw attention to instances in which children have made such equivalent trains, perhaps asking them what they think will happen with other pairs of rods. Later, interpretations in terms of numbers gives one statements such as $3 + 4 = 4 + 3$.

It seems important to note at this point how valuable the use of the rods can be in general in helping to formulate children's perceptions about the structure of number. To do justice to the enormous potential of the rods would take a lot of space, however, and there is no room for such in depth treatment here. The interested reader should refer to Gattegno (1957), Gattegno (1963) and Goutard (1964). There are references in more modern books, but these are the original texts written about Cuisenaire rods and in many ways they are the best. They stress the idea of 'algebra before arithmetic' and the importance of working with perceptual experiences.

Incidental awareness

Awareness of the commutativity of addition could arise informally through lots of other activities. We have already seen it arise in the context of building up the set of additions to a particular total (see p.). Another similar situation arises from inviting children to colour in spots in arrangements such as that shown in figure 3.15, suggesting (amongst other things, perhaps) that they see how many spots have been coloured in on the left hand side, how many on the right hand side, and how many altogether. 5 year old Sam found that he had coloured 5 spots altogether with 1 spot on the left hand side and 4 spots on the right hand side; and the same with 4 spots on the left hand side and 1 spot on the right hand side.

Figure 3.15

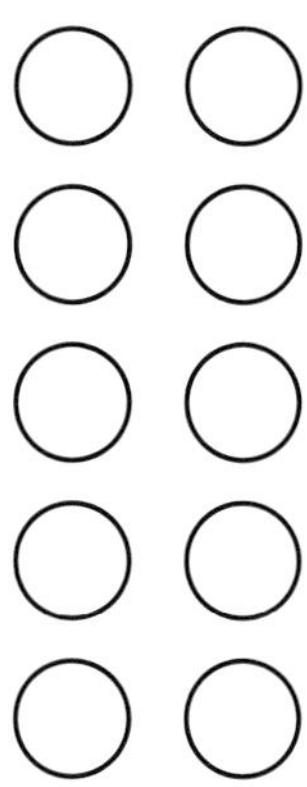

Making up sums

As well as the commutativity of addition arising incidentally as in the activities mentioned above, activities can be devised to focus on it overtly. For example, try asking children to make up an addition and work out the answer, then to turn the sum back to front and work out the answer again. What do they notice? Does it always work?

Before working out the second addition in each pair of sums, children could be invited to say what they think will happen. This not only involves them in prediction, it should also help keep them in an active stance towards the activity, otherwise it would be easy to carry out the pairs of sums with little thought towards the significance.

Why not give them calculators so that they can try out additions of numbers as large as they like? This could play an important part in them coming to realize that the rule works for any pair of numbers.

A case study of children working on the activity is included at the end of this chapter.

Other laws

Some children might be able to carry out a similar activity to the last one described but using multiplication instead of addition. This could be linked to incidental perceptions of, say, the fact that the pencil rack can be thought of as 3 rows of 4 pencils or 4 rows of 3 pencils; 2 groups of 3 children involves as many individuals as 3 groups of 2 children etc.

Given a sum such as 6 + 2 + 1, some children might well work out the 2 + 1 = 3, first, then tackle 6 + 3. Other children's attention could be drawn to this: does it matter, then, which two numbers are added first in such an addition? Such discussions could lead young children to an informal awareness of what we would term the 'associativity of addition', that is that (a + b) + c is the same as a + (b + c).

As an example of the sort of thinking which can be carried out round a three part addition, consider the following snippet of conversation between Richard (aged 5/6) and I when he was working out 4 + 3 + 2:

Richard: Add 2 to the 3, so that makes 5 and so add 4 ...
9.

MB: Can you think of a different way to do it?

Richard: Maybe if we add the 2 to the 4 so that means ...
6 ..., then 3, so that makes ... 9 altogether.
9 again!

MB Can you think of any other way?

Richard: 3 add to the 4 so that's 7 and then ... 8, 9 ...
so it's 9.

THE NATIONAL CURRICULUM FOR KEY STAGE 1 MATHEMATICS

The activities discussed in the first two sections of this chapter all centre on the recognition and use of odd and even numbers. In terms of the National Curriculum, this relates directly to 'recognise sequences, including odd and even numbers' (from Number: 2a)

The activities in the third section are connected with 'learn multiplication and division facts relating to the 2s, 5s, 10s' (from Number: 3c).

The main subject of the fourth and fifth sections, namely the commutativity of addition, is an example of a general principle which it is important for children to grasp. In terms of the National Curriculum, it concerns 'Understand general statements ... and investigate whether particular cases match them' (Using and Applying Mathematics: 4c). It also relates to 'explore and record patterns in addition and subtraction' (from Number: 3b) and 'recognise simple patterns and relationships and make related predictions about them' (Using and Applying Mathematics: 4a).

These last three items from the Programme of Study also feature heavily within the activities from the rest of the chapter.

There are also a lot of opportunities for pupils to:

> 'explain their thinking to support the development of their reasoning' (Using and Applying Mathematics: 1b);
>
> learn to 'understand the language of number' (Using and Applying Mathematics: 3a);
>
> 'discuss their work, responding to and asking mathematical questions' (Using and Applying Mathematics: 3c);
>
> 'ask questions including "What would happen if?" and "Why?"' (Using and Applying Mathematics: 4b);
>
> 'count orally up to 10 and beyond' (from Number: 2a);
>
> learn to 'know addition and subtraction facts to 20' (from Number: 3c);

Other parts of the Programme of Study may well feature in particular activities. As examples:

> Comparing arrangements of counters in the 'A grid activity' (p 55) provides an opportunity for pupils to 'describe positions, using common words; recognise movements in a straight line, ie translations, and rotations...' (from Shape, Space and Measures: 3a).

The activity 'Making two equal piles' (p 52) might involve children in developing their understanding of 'half' and this addresses 'recognise and use in context simple fractions, including halves ...' (from Number: 2c).
Sorting numbers into those which are in the 2 x table and those which are in the 5 x table (see 'A collection game' p 62) is an activity in which the children will 'sort and classify a set of objects using criteria related to their properties' (Number: 5a). Deciding in which tables the different numbers occur, could involve knowledge of the 'patterns of multiples ... explaining their patterns and using them to make predictions' (from Number: 3b).
When using calculators to make up sums to test the commutativity of addition, children are likely to try out large numbers and hence to 'encounter numbers greater than 1000' (Number: 1b). The following references to calculators also apply: 'use a basic calculator, reading the display' (Number: 3e) and 'use calculators both as a means to explore number and as a tool for calculating with realistic data, eg numbers with several digits' (Number: 1d).

Case study: Distinguishing between odds and evens and investigating their appearance in different grids

I showed a group of four 5/6 year olds a small book but said that we were going to do something strange with it: we were not going to read it but look for numbers on the pages. I opened the book and asked if the children could see any numbers. Andrew pointed to one at the top right and Louise pointed to one at the top left. Louise added that one was number 5 and the other number 4.

Michelle opened the book in a different place. The children saw where the numbers were. Paul said 'There's more of them!' with some surprise. Those numbers were larger but Louise correctly identified them as 14 and 15.

I turned the book to the front and said that we would look through all the numbers. As I turned the pages the children said the numbers. When they had reached 10, I asked them what they could say about all the numbers so far. Michelle said 'There's all the numbers.' I asked if they were 'all over the place'. Quite emphatically, Michelle said that they were not and added 'They go 1, 2, 3, 4, 5, 6, 7, 8, 9, 10' very quickly, perhaps drawing attention to the familiar order of the set. Continuing through the rest of the numbers past 10 revealed that the two girls had a good recognition of and knowledge of number names for the numerals 11 to 20, whereas the boys did not. Louise's grasp seemed even more secure than Michelle's, whereas Paul's seemed less secure than Andrew's.

The last number in the book was 20, at the top of the left hand side of the last page. However, the children looked at the top right hand side of the inside of the back cover, obviously expecting there to be a number there too! They were amused to find nothing written there but when asked why that might be so, Paul said 'It isn't a proper page.' Louise added that it was cardboard. I asked if anyone could think which number would be on there if the numbering continued. Louise correctly suggested 21.

I said that now we had seen all the numbers on the pages we would just concentrate on some of them. Opening the book at random, I commented on one of the numbers being on the right hand side and one on the left hand side. I said that, first of all, we would see which numbers were on the right hand side, then we would look at the left hand side.

As the children together identified the numbers on the right hand sides of the pages, I asked them to find them on a number ladder and mark them in some way. Andrew made the very sensible suggestion that the numbers on one side of the book could be written on that side of the number ladder and likewise those on the other. All the children adopted this positioning idea. Andrew, Michelle and Louise re-wrote the numbers on the appropriate side, whilst Paul drew a little diagonal line.

After Louise had marked several 'right' numbers on her ladder, she noticed that they were going in a pattern. I asked if she could guess ahead to where the next 'right' number would be. She guessed '9' and was delighted to find that this was correct. The others started to make predictions too. Andrew was unable to give the numeral its correct name in each case but could either point to it or refer to it as, for example, 'one and five' (15). Paul made some rather bizarre predictions, pointing, for example, to 12 after he had filled in 11 and 13. By the time he had reached the end of the ladder he still seemed either unaware of the pattern or unable to control the production of it. I made a mental note to observe his future pattern work carefully.

When Andrew had finished marking on the 'right' numbers, he suggested colouring the spaces on the ladder. This seemed a good way of making clear which numbers should be marked and which not, particularly in Andrew's case as he had made a few errors and, although he had crossed these out, at a glance it was not very clear which numbers were meant to be marked and which were not. All the children coloured in the 'right' numbers in red.

I asked if any of them were aware of another name for these 'right' or 'red' numbers. No one made any suggestions except Michelle who started saying the names again of the individual numbers. I mentioned that the numbers were called 'odd' numbers. This term did not seem to be familiar to any of the group.

Next the children concentrated on the left hand numbers. Having found them all on their number ladders, they coloured the spaces in blue. I mentioned the term 'even' and, again, no one seemed familiar with this.

As an example of one of the completed ladders, see Andrew's in figure 3.16. A brief explanation of Andrew's numbering seems called for: working on the odd numbers he wrote the numerals 1 to 11 correctly at first, but then recorded 13, 15, 17 and 19 as 3, 5, 7 and 9. Michelle noticed this and said that there should be 'a 1 on them'. It seems that Andrew obliged, not only writing a 1 by each of those numbers but also against the numbers he had already copied from the book correctly! It is to be noted, however, that he tackled the even numbers much better.

Figure 3.16

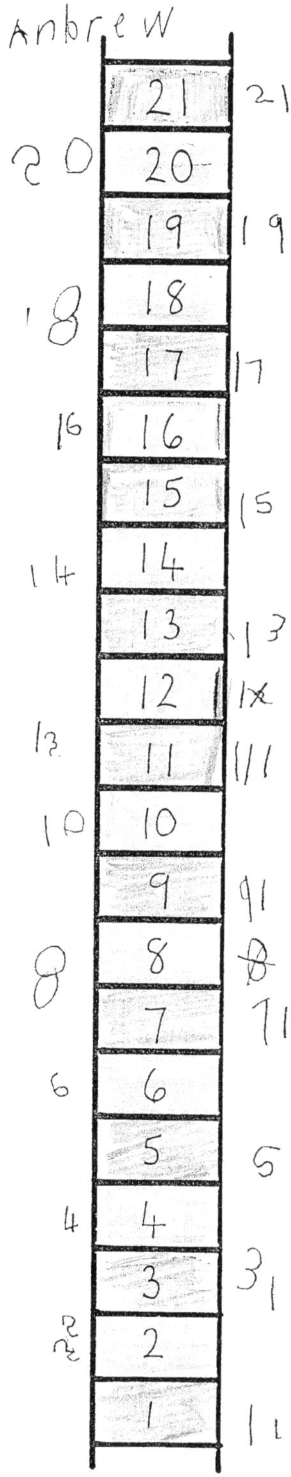

As the children finished their number ladders, I gave them a grid with the numbers 1 to 20 on it, arranged in 5 columns. They talked about where the numbers went, reading them through in order from line to line: 1,2,3,4,5; 6,7,8,9,10; etc. I asked each child to choose either the red, odd numbers or the blue, even numbers and find them on the new grid, colouring them in.

Michelle and Louise tackled this task quickly and competently. Pointing to the diagonal lines of her red pattern, Louise said it was 'like a triangle' and 'like a kite': some interesting imagery here!

Andrew found the task quite difficult, colouring in several squares red when they should have been blue. I looked at a couple of examples with him: having located a red section of the number ladder, he sometimes seemed to find it difficult to find the number on the grid and coloured a different square by mistake. He looked for numbers at random unlike the two girls who went through the numbers in order starting at the foot of the ladder.

Despite Paul's original difficulties in seeing how the patterns were building up on the number ladder, he tackled the grid colouring slowly but competently and became aware of a pattern in his blue, even numbers. He worked methodically, going backwards from 20. His work is shown in figure 3.17.

Figure 3.17

When the children had finished their grids, I invited them to make up their own grids with a different number of numbers going across. They then looked for either the red, odd numbers or the blue, even ones in these new grids. I suggested that they keep to the same sort of numbers as before so that they could compare their results.

Andrew chose 7 numbers going across for his new grid. I was pleased to note that, this time, he made only one mistake: he coloured the 12 red when it should have been left blank. Later, Paul noticed the mistake, shouting to Andrew 'Here ... you shouldn't have coloured one, two, that's an evil (sic) number!' I was surprised by the confidence expressed in this announcement and amused by the use of 'evil'! When I mentioned that the word was really 'even', Paul said it out loud several times but I heard him still saying 'evil' later on!

Paul himself chose 6 numbers going across for his new grid. He found out that

2
8
14
20

were each coloured in blue and commented that they were 'all in a row'. Having identified the other even numbers in the top line going across the grid, he used his 'row' idea to help complete some of the other vertical lines of blue colouring, guessing which numbers would be so coloured and checking to see if they were.

Louise chose 10 and then 8 squares across for her own grids. She found that the pattern of the red, odd numbers in these looked like each other but not like the pattern in the first (5) grid. Her work is shown in figure 3.18.

Michelle completed new grids with 9, 3 and 4 squares in them. She found that the pattern of blue, even squares was the same for the 5, 9 and 3 grids but different for the 4 grid which in turn was like Michelle's 10 and 8 grids.

Figure 3.18

Figure 3.18 cont

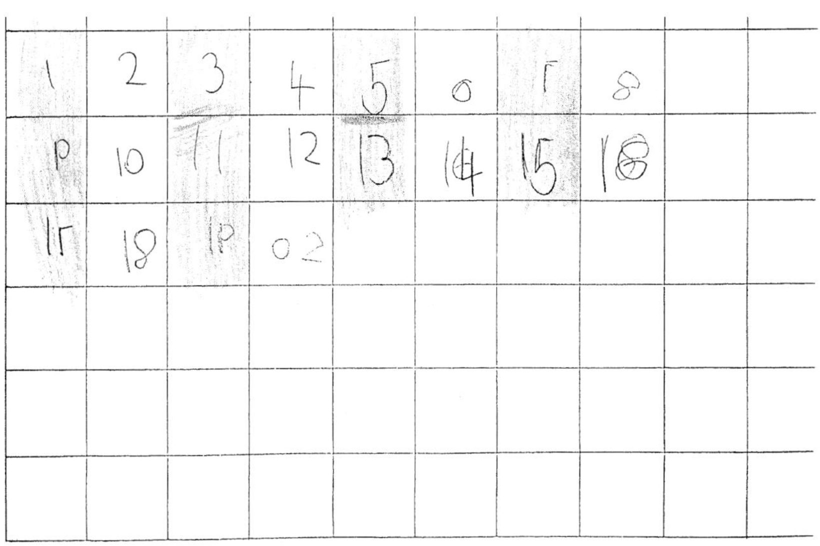

Case study: Turning sums back to front

I asked each member of a group of four 6/7 year olds to make up and write down an addition sum. Kellie-Anne chose 5+1, Daniel 5+6, Joanne 5+2 and Brett 16+11. The first three worked out the answers to theirs immediately, but Brett said he was not sure that he could do his. I offered him a calculator to use, which he did, but before he had arrived at the answer Daniel announced that it would be 27!

Then I asked the children to write their sums the other way round so that if they had started with, say, 3+6 they would now write 6+3. As they were writing, I asked them what they thought the answers would be. Kellie-Anne, Daniel and Joanne said that their answers would be the same as before (but were they actually working these out rather than predicting ahead?) whereas Brett did not think that his answer would be. When he tried it out on his calculator he seemed very surprised to find that it was the same!

I wondered what the other children would make of larger numbers. I gave them each a calculator and suggested that they try out 'bigger numbers like Brett's'. Kellie-Anne started with 13+10, Daniel 16+11 (Brett's original choice), Joanne 15+12 and Brett 100+1000(!).

After Kellie-Anne had found that 13+10 worked, she said that she thought it always would but went on to try other numbers including ones that she thought were 'harder', namely 70+52 and 200+400. See figure 3.19 for Kellie-Anne's written record of her work.

Figure 3.19

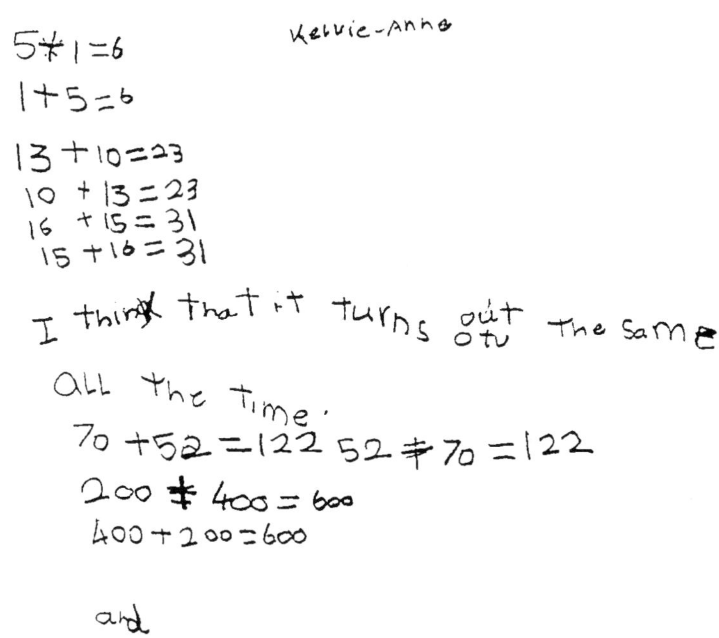

After writing down and recording the answer to Brett's original sum, Daniel tried 511+100. He was surprised to find that it did give the same answer when reversed. Like Kellie-Anne, he also went on to try "harder" sums, including 800+9700. He found that the pairs of additions all gave the same answer but was not convinced that it would always work. See figure 3.20 for Daniel's work.

Figure 3.20

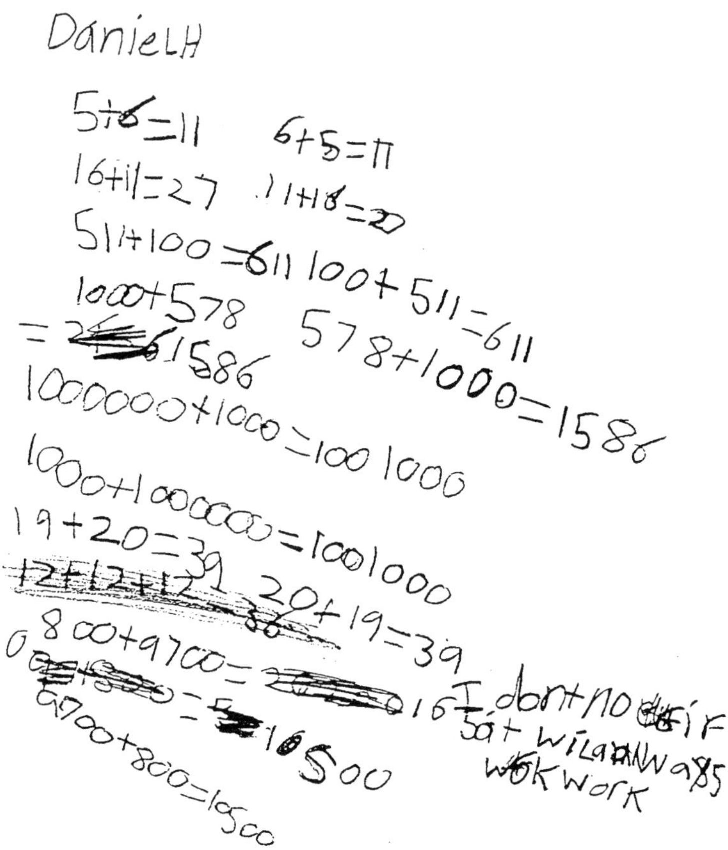

Joanne said that she thought it would keep on happening. Amongst the sums she tried she wrote 200+200, then was very amused to find that it would not make any difference if she turned it round! See figure 3.21.

Figure 3.21

Joanne

5 + _ = 7   2 + 5 = 7

15 + 12 = 27   12 + 15 = 27

16 + 10 = 26   10 + 16 = 26

I thoaght that it was going to
Be the same ~~but~~ it was
and
200 + 200 400
if I turned it roud it will be
The sam agen

200 + 800 = 1000 I think
800 and 200 is going to be
The same
800 + 200 = 1000

Brett did not think his 100+1000 would work but was pleased when it did. See figure 3.22. I wondered if he knew what the words were for '100', '1000' and '1100'. I asked him and he told me 'a hundred' and 'a thousand' correctly but was unsure about the last number. I told him that this was 'One thousand, one hundred' and commented on it making sense because he had put a thousand and a hundred together. He then asked how to write a million and was amused when I told him that it had six noughts! He used a million in his next pair of sums, together with a thousand, and was delighted by the size of the answers and that they were the same!. I asked him if he could read this new number. Again he was not sure, but when I asked him what he had added to obtain it he seemed to make the connection and eventually read it off as 'a million , a thousand'. I made a mental note that it would be interesting to see if he could work out how to read other similar numbers later.

Figure 3.22

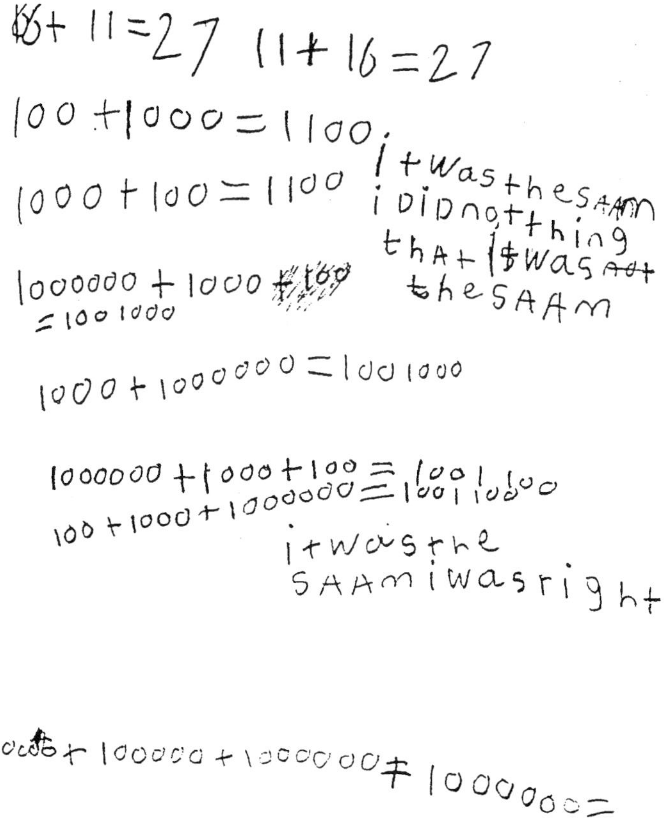

For his next addition, Brett decided to try three numbers and chose a million, a thousand and a hundred. By this time he seemed convinced that the answers would be the same in any case. At the end of the session he wrote down a million four times but then realized he would have exactly the same string of numbers when they were turned round!

It seemed important to end the session with a comment about the answers for pairs of additions appearing always to be the same, but that Daniel was right still to be hesitant. I was careful not to imply that we could be certain that the process would always work, because we had been generalizing from examples without seeking any underlying reason why it should be so.

Notes

1. Children can encounter problems deciding how zero and one fit in various situations. As examples: (1) Is 0 an odd or an even number? (2) Is 1 a prime number? Deciding on answers to such questions can involve children in important mathematical processes, for instance seeing if patterns already established with the other counting numbers could be continued to incorporate the number under question sensibly. Deciding how to colour and classify a one-square strip in the coloured strips activity, is one of these sorts of situations and it is worthy of note that this arose with children as young as 4/5 years and that they then engaged in quite a sophisticated debate about the problem.

Chapter Four: Rules

Chapter 2 was concerned with the generation of and recognition of patterns in various simple number situations. There is, however, a further concept implicit in 'Understanding relationships between numbers' which has not been brought to the fore yet. This is the notion of a rule.

Consider the following example:

1 5
2 6
3 7
4 8
5 9

Here we have taken a starting set of numbers 1, 2, 3, 4, 5, applied a particular rule to each member of the set and ended up with a second set of numbers: 5, 6, 7, 8, 9. In this case we can see that the rule was 'add 4'.

Using rules and finding which rules have been used is a very fundamental part of mathematics. Young children can be involved in meaningful activities, based on using and finding rules, which engage them in recognising simple patterns and relationships, provide a vehicle for making and testing preditions, and give rise to general statements and the posing of questions such as 'Does it always work?' and 'Why does it happen?'

Using repeated shape patterns

Much of the early work on rules can centre on counting different attributes of simple, repeated, geometric shapes. For example, in strips such as those shown in figure 4.1, children could count and compare the number of squares with the number of triangles. The results of the examples in the diagram are

Number of squares	Number of triangles
4	8
6	12
2	4
7	14

and it can be seen that the number of triangles is obtained by doubling the number of squares.

Figure 4.1

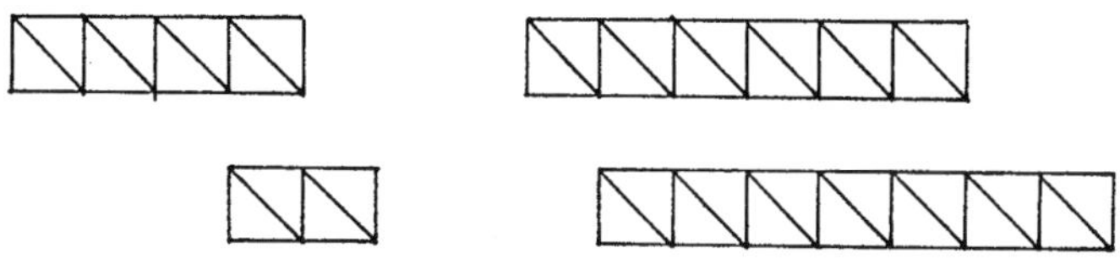

Instead of contriving examples such as the above, teachers can seize upon examples as they occur naturally and focus the children's attention on the rule-finding aspects of the situations. For example, when a group of 6/7 year olds were making patterns with tissue paper circles, the teacher noticed that some of the children had included lines of overlapping circles on their sheets, such as in figure 4.2. She asked the children how many circles and how many overlaps there were for particular examples the children had devised and the children noticed that there was 'one less' overlap than circles each time. They were able to predict how many overlaps there would be for 10 circles and then for their own choices of numbers of circles, realizing that they needed to 'take one off' in each case.

Figure 4.2

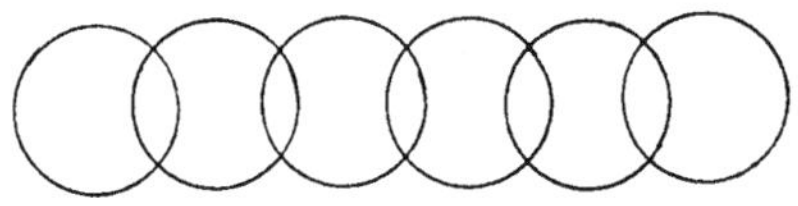

Trying to make predictions can help focus children's attention on what the rule is, if they have not already found it from the starting examples. By its very nature, making predictions also takes the children beyond what is given, involving them in pushing forward their thinking beyond the observation of actual objects. Children often delight in making predictions for numbers which they consider to be really large, for instance the number of overlaps for a thousand circles, to continue the example above. Such use of large numbers can contribute greatly towards young children's growing confidence and feelings of control over the number systems.

The following are examples of some objects which have attributes which can be compared and for which children could imagine bigger or smaller sized objects:

(1) A ladder. Compare rungs and spaces. What would happen with larger or smaller ladders?

(2) A radiator. Compare the 'ridges' with the spaces between them. What would happen with other sizes?

(3) A book case. Compare the number of shelves with the number of spaces. What would happen with other sizes?

Designs on wallpaper, fabrics, greetings cards and pottery etc. may well yield possibilities for other rule-finding activities. For example, the numbers of berries for different numbers of holly leaves could be considered in the repeating pattern from the borders of a Christmas card shown in figure 4.3.

A case study of children comparing the number of rungs and spaces in different length ladders is given at the end of this chapter.

Figure 4.3

Machines

Early ideas about functions can emerge sensibly in the context of using a machine, both actual and imagined. Some examples of possible activities follow.

What is my rule?

The heart of this activity is that child A enters a number in a calculator, then passes it to child B who carries out an operation on the number and passes the calculator back to A. A has to try to work out what the operation was.

This is quite a well known activity and has a fair amount of potential. In its simplest form as written above, it provides children with opportunities to think about which operations it is sensible to suggest and opportunities to carry out arithmetic, most likely mentally, whilst assessing the likely success of a particular guess. Points might also arise such as the fact that two different operations fit particular situations, for example, if 6 comes out as 3 then this could be because the operation was 'subtract 3' or 'divide by 2'. Children can also be encouraged to think which operations they would need to go back from the finishing number to the starting number. This would provide some early experience of inverse operations.

More exciting possibilities exist if child B carries out two operations on child A's choice of numbers. Such combination of operations is likely to be much more difficult to detect than a single operation. Ambiguities can often be resolved by child B giving child A more than one number to process.

In some situations, there may be more than one combination of operations which fits all the outputs from child A's inputs of numbers. For example, suppose B decides to add 10 then subtract 4. Add 9, subtract 3; add 11, subtract 5; add 20, subtract 14; etc. would work equally as well. In such circumstances children could explore how many different solutions exist and they might well find that, in some cases, the possibilities are endless.

The program 'Flags' on the microcomputer utilizes the same sort of idea of involving children in guessing which operations are being used to obtain numbers from others.

Trying out double functions

Instead of trying to work out someone else's choice of functions, children could be involved in exploring the result of carrying out a particular combination of two functions on numbers of their choice.

Opportunities for a lot of pattern-spotting are afforded by this activity. This is particularly the case if children choose their starting numbers in some sort of order, for example, increasing or decreasing consecutively, going up or down in twos etc. Indeed, children may well learn from this activity that the imposition of some sort of structure on their choice of starting numbers provides richer potential than a random choice does.

Children could pretend that the combination of operations is achieved by putting together two machines. They can make up their own combination of machines to try out. A case study of children working on this interpretation of the activity is included at the end of the chapter.

A rich variety of follow up activities are possible. Some could be centred around the following suggestions/questions:

> Does it make any difference if the two machines are switched round? For which machines does it matter? ... does it not matter?
>
> Choose the output for your machines, then work out what the input would have to be.
>
> Choose a set of numbers with a common difference for the input, for example, 3, 5, 7, 9, 11. What is the difference between the numbers in the output? Repeat for other sets of numbers with other common differences. Any rules?
>
> Try making up some pairs of machines whose combined output is the same as the input.

LOGO

There is not room here to do justice to the rich learning potential of involving children in using turtle graphics. However, in the context of 'functions', it seems appropriate to mention that each instruction such as FORWARD 11, RIGHT 90 etc. can be viewed as an operation and that as pupils design and make their own pictures and patterns they will be finding more and more about how these operations behave. This could include points such as discovering that FORWARD 300, BACK 100 puts the turtle in the same place as FORWARD 200 would have done; that FORWARD 100, BACK 100 takes the turtle back to the beginning; and that RIGHT 180 gives the same result as LEFT 180 etc. Similar discoveries can be made when working with a robot such as ROMA. Children's growing awareness of the nature of the operations and their interconnections helps them gain increasing control over programming the robot to carry out what they require.

Worthy of note, too (though, strictly speaking, more closely connected with the themes of the first two chapters that with this one), is the fact that the use of LOGO graphics can open up another mode for exploring number patterns. Suppose we make up a repeating number pattern such as 3,4,1,3,4,1,3,4,1... then decide that each number will become the amount the turtle moves forward, turning through 90 clockwise after each such operation.[2]

This gives us

FORWARD 3
RIGHT 90
FORWARD 4
RIGHT 90
FORWARD 1
RIGHT 90

to be repeated as many times as we wish. This particular set of instructions gives us the arrangement in figure 4.4. Theresa (7/8 years) found that the set of instructions had to be carried out just 4 times to complete the diagram and went on to try out 3,5,1 and 3,6,1 similarly repeated 4 times each. She became interested in seeing what happened in the centre of each pattern and correctly predicted the centre of the arrangement for 3,7,1. Her own drawings of the patterns on squared paper are shown in figure 4.5.

(N.B. Some versions of LOGO will need larger numbers for the FORWARD operations to be seen clearly.)

Figure 4.4

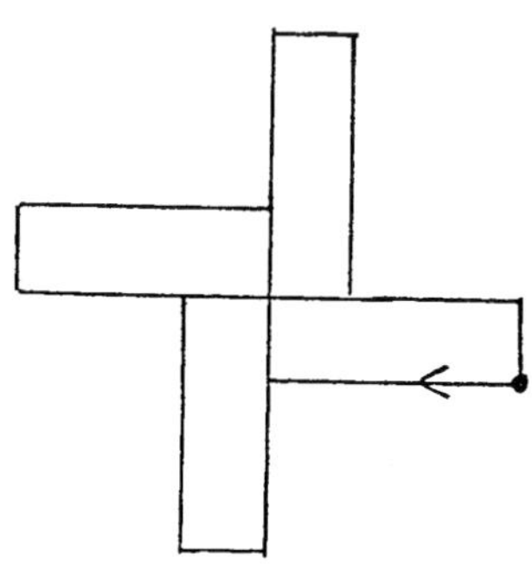

Figure 4.5

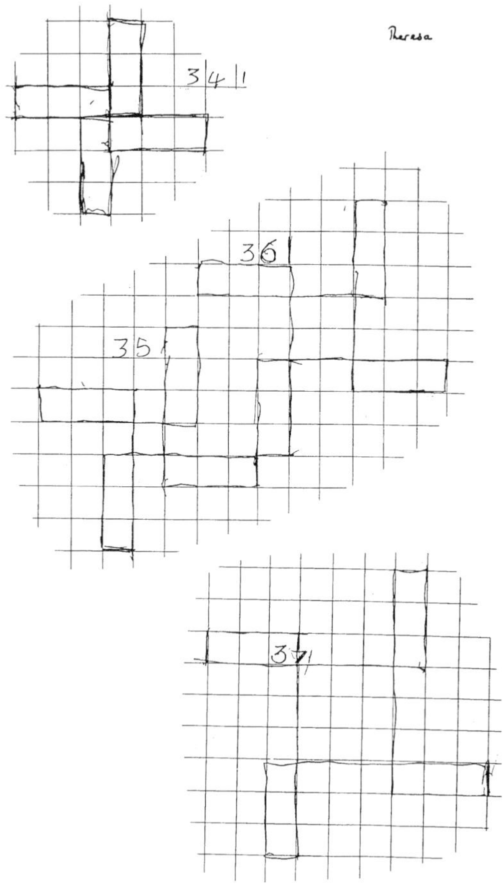

Cardboard machines

Children often seem to enjoy working with 'pretend machines' made by fixing together two discs of card with a split pin through their centres and with two 'windows' in the top disc as in figure 4.6. Numbers written on the bottom disc act as the input when they appear in the left hand window of the top disc. Numbers appearing in the right hand window act as the output. For example, the machine might be an 'add 4' machine in which case as the number 1 appears in the left hand window, 5 appears on the right hand side.

Such machines can be used in various ways. For example, the right hand window can be covered temporarily and children asked to work out the output themselves, then check their results by seeing what was in the window. Whilst this sort of activity can provide useful practice in developing the idea of inputs and outputs and in reinforcing number bonds, it seems of little further value. However, such a closed activity can easily be turned into a more open one by giving children the opportunity to create their own function machines, that is to choose their own operations and inputs to go on the cardboard shell.

Often children will be quite ambitious in their choice of operations. For example, having used machines whose operations were additions and subtractions of numbers below 10, Rebecca (6/7 years) chose 'add 19' for her own machine. Similarly, children might set themselves large numbers for the input. For example, Paul (6/7 years) incorporated 100, 102, 200, 1000, 500 and 12000 amongst the numbers in his input to an 'add 9' machine.

Sometimes, children insert numbers in the input in consecutive order. For instance, in her 'add 14' machine, Claire (6/7 years) wrote in the numbers consecutively from 1 to 13. At first sight, one might think this is a shame from the point of view that she is not going to have to think much about each output, she can just add on 1 to the previous value all the time. However, we must remember that for young children, the fact that the output can be generated in this way could itself be an interesting discovery. This was certainly true in Claire's case. She worked out 1 + 14 = 15, 2 + 14 = 16, 3 + 14 = 17 and only then realized what was happening to the output and why that was the case. She was delighted with her discovery!

Sometimes, children choose inputs to which they think at first there is no output. This is what happened when Peter (8 years) chose 1 as an input to his 'subtract 5' machine. In such circumstances, children might decide to change the input to something for which an obvious output is available, or the situation might be ripe for the introduction of a new sort of number, that is negative numbers in this particular case, though not necessarily named as such. Peter originally thought that 0 might be the answer to 1 - 5, but was not very happy about it and was even less so when asked if all of 2 - 5, 3 - 5, 4 - 5 and 5 - 5 would be 0 too. He said he thought that 4 - 5 should be smaller than 0 and 3 - 5 smaller than that. He saw that 4 - 5 should be '1 smaller than 0', 3 - 5 '2 smaller than 0' etc. and invented the symbolism 1s, 2s etc. to record this. On a later occasion, he perceived a connection between his 's numbers' and the numbers below zero on a thermometer.

Children can swop their machines so that they can work at ones which others have constructed. This sometimes highlights mistakes made by the originator of the machine and discrepancies can be discussed and put right!

Figure 4.6

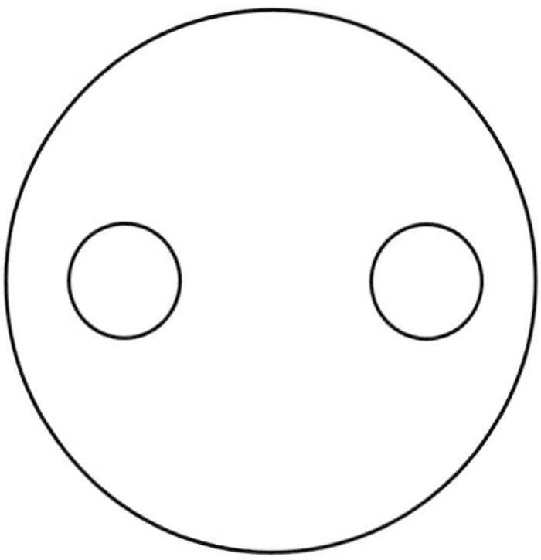

THE NATIONAL CURRICULUM FOR KEY STAGE 1 MATHEMATICS

The activities discussed in the 'Using repeated shape patterns' section (p 81) are centred on requiring children to 'recognise simple patterns and relationships and make related predictions about them' (Using and Applying Mathematics: 4a). The children will also need to 'count orally up to 10 and beyond, knowing the number names; count collections of objects ... (from Number: 2a). And there will be opportunities to 'describe and discuss shapes and patterns that can be seen or visualised' (Shape, Space and Measures: 2a) and 'recognise and use the geometrical features of shapes ...' (from Shape, Space and Measures: 2c).

In the 'What is my rule?' activity (p 84), the children will need to test out different number operations in trying to determine the rule. This is concerned with the children learning to 'understand the operations of addition, subtraction as taking away and comparison, and the relationship between them, recognise situations to which they apply ...' (from Number: 4a) and 'understand the operations of multiplication and division ...' (from Number: 4b). Thinking which operations are required to go back from the finishing number to the starting number may well involve children in an awareness of 'the fact that subtraction is the inverse of addition' (from Number: 3d). As various number bonds will be required, 'know addition and subtraction facts to 20' (from Number: 3c) will also feature.

In the activities 'Trying out double operations' (p 84) and 'Cardboard machines' (p 87), all of the National Curriculum statements just listed for the 'What is my rule?' activity will again be appropriate. There is added emphasis on pattern spotting in 'Trying out double operations' too, and hence with 'explore and record patterns in addition and subtraction, and then patterns of multiples ...' (from Number: 3b) and 'recognise simple patterns and relationships and make related predictions about them' (Using and Applying Mathematics: 4a). For some children, these latter two items might also be addressed within the 'Cardboard machines' activity.

In making predictions for their own choice of numbers in the 'Using repeated shape patterns' activity, children often choose large numbers and may thus 'encounter numbers greater than 1000' (Number: 1b). Similarly, there is scope for children to choose large numbers as input for their cardboard machines and as input for the combination of machines in the 'Trying out double operations'.

In the 'LOGO' activity (p 85), the children will be required to 'use repeating patterns to develop ideas of regularity and sequencing' (Number: 3a). The whole of Shape, Space and Measures: 3a and 3b will also be appropriate, namely 'describe positions, using common words; recognise movements in a straight line, ie translations, and rotations, and combine them in simple ways; copy, continue and make patterns' (3a) and 'understand angle as a measure of turn and recognise quarter-turns and half-turns; recognise right angles' (3b).

'Use a basic calculator, reading the display' (Number: 3e) also features in the 'What is my rule?' activity.

Some items from the Using and Applying Mathematics section of the Programme of Study have been mentioned in conjunction with specific activities above. The following are also relevant across all the activities:

> 'Use and apply mathematics in practical tasks, in real-life problems and within mathematics itself' (1a);
>
> 'Explain their thinking to support the development of their reasoning' (1b);
>
> 'Organise and check their work' (2d);
>
> 'Understand the language of number ... ' (from 3a);
>
> 'Relate numerals and other mathematical symbols, eg '+', '=', to a range of situations' (3b);
>
> 'Discuss their work, responding to and asking mathematical questions' (3c);
>
> 'Use a variety of forms of mathematical presentation' (3d);
>
> 'Ask questions including "What would happen if?" and "Why?"' (4b);
>
> 'Understand general statements and investigate whether particular cases match them' (4c).

Case study: Ladders

I asked the group of five 6/7 year olds who had been playing the ladders game described in chapter 5 (see p.), to look at one of the ladders on the board. Katy chose the ladder going diagonally from 63 to 85, identifying it by pointing to it. When asked to count how many rungs there were in the ladder, Christopher made it 9 correctly. When asked to count how many spaces there were, Amanda made it 10. I noted that she was counting the areas beyond the rungs at each end. I had anticipated that the children would just count the spaces between the rungs. I decided not to comment at this stage, wondering if we would end up with two different sets of data which might provide extra food for thought.

I said that I would like the children each to choose some more ladders from the board, or to make up some of their own, counting how many rungs and spaces there were in each one. I suggested that they drew the ladders on pieces of plain paper, 'so that we can see which you choose'. The children had no difficulty starting on this and were able to be left on their own.

Continuing as she had begun, Amanda counted the areas outside the rungs too. She produced ladders with 17, 3 and 14 rungs and hence 18, 4 and 15 spaces, all of which she counted correctly. See figure 4.7.

Figure 4.7

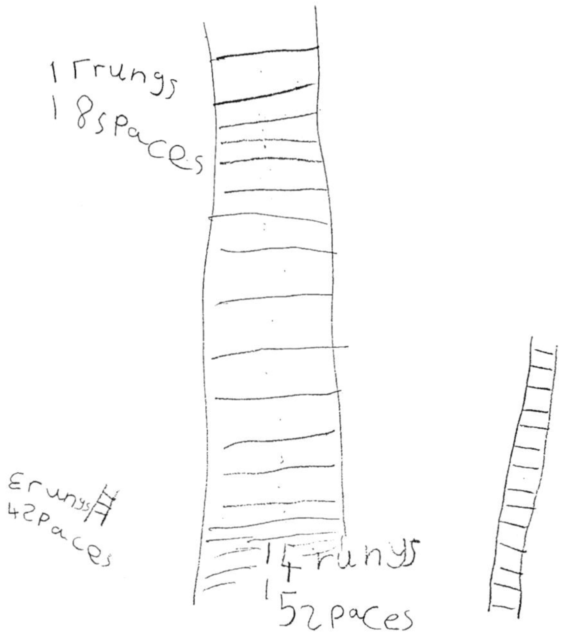

Figure 4.8

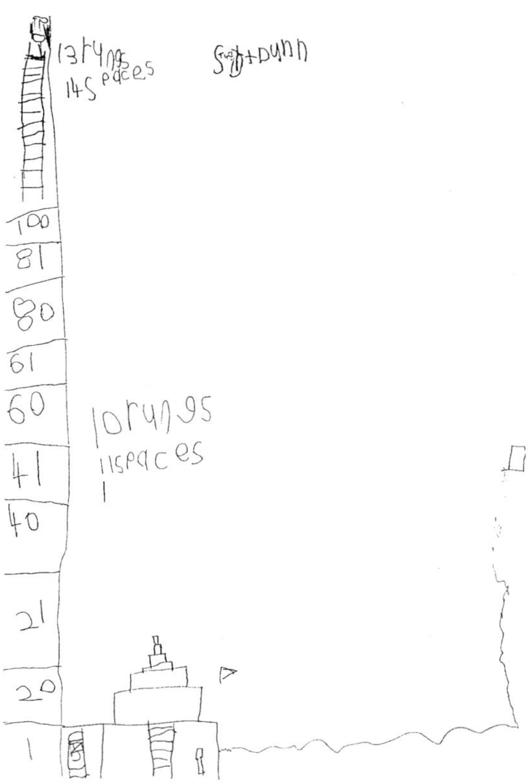

Stuart also counted the end spaces. He drew ladders with 10 and 13 rungs, thus obtaining 11 and 14 spaces. I noticed that he was not concentrating on the task all the time, but did keep coming back to it. As can be seen from figure 4.8, Stuart copied some numbers from the ladders game board too. He also drew some extra pieces at the bottom of his sheet which he later told me were like a game he had at home!

Katy, Christopher and Michael each counted just the spaces inside the rungs of their ladders. Michael produced a ladder with 14 rungs and 13 spaces and another with 3 rungs and 2 spaces. See figure 4.9. He was called out of the classroom for a while and so was unable to complete more examples.

Figure 4.9

As can be seen from figure 4.10, Katy drew ladders with 24 rungs, 23 spaces; 27 rungs, 26 spaces; and 6 rungs, 5 spaces. She also completed one with 17 rungs and 16 spaces but, by accident, she recorded this as 16 rungs and 17 spaces at first. Looking back at these figures later, she expressed some surprise and said that 17 was 'bigger' but it should have been smaller! This prompted her to recount both the rungs and the spaces and she found that she had put the numbers the wrong way round. She drew a line from the 16 to where she had written 'spaces' and one from the 17 to where she had written 'rungs' to indicate that the numbers should be swopped over. However, she decided that this was still not very clear, crossed it all out, and re-wrote it correctly above her original writing.

Figure 4.10

Christopher drew a ladder with an amazing number of rungs! See figure 4.11. He asked me to help him count them. I moved my pencil slowly up the ladder whilst he counted. He was uncertain of some of the tens words ('thirty', 'forty' etc.), but could take over with 'thirty-one', 'thirty-two' etc. once the tens word had been supplied. He was very excited when he got to 70 and said he knew how to write it. We repeated the activity for the number of spaces and again he was delighted with the result.

Figure 4.11

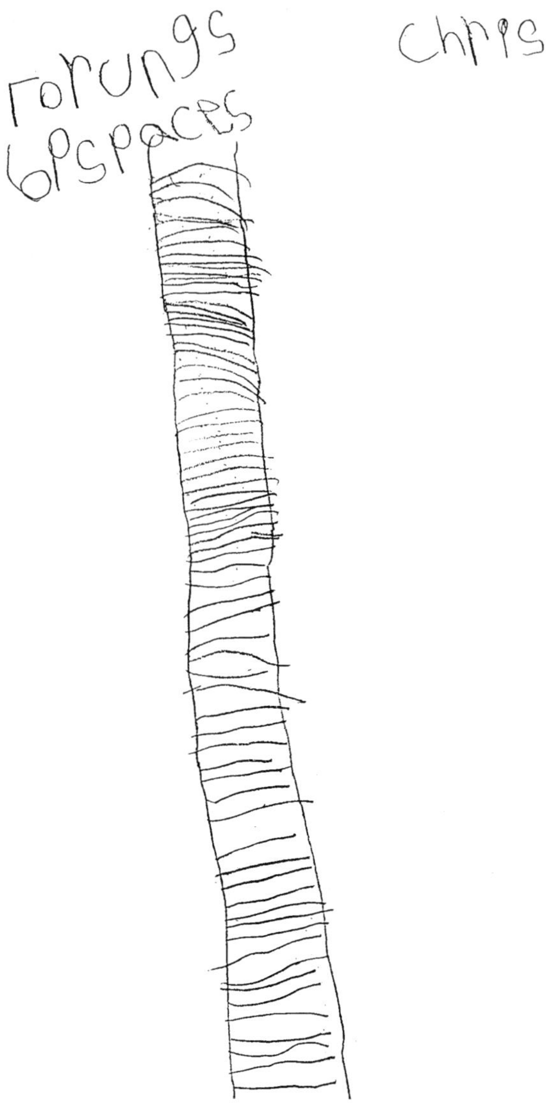

Once the children had completed the ladders shown in figures 4.7 to 4.11, I said that perhaps we could put the results together to see if there was anything to notice about them. I asked Katy, Michael and Christopher to give me their numbers, confining this request to those three for the present because of realizing that Stuart and Amanda had counted the spaces differently. In front of the children I recorded the results as follows:

Rungs	Spaces
24	23
70	69
6	5
27	26
14	13

and asked the group if they noticed anything. Stuart said 'They're going backwards'. The others seemed to agree. I invited them to guess a number of rungs. Katy suggested 100. I asked how many spaces they thought that would give. Christopher said 99. I asked for another suggestion for a number of rungs. Amanda said 98 and some of the others quickly worked out that there should be 97 spaces. The third suggestion was put forward by Christopher: 1000 rungs! No one seemed very sure how many spaces that would create and the numbers eventually offered included 199 and 1001. I took out a calculator and asked Katy to put in 1000 which she did correctly. I asked what we would need to do to see which number was 'going backwards' from 1000 and added that that meant which number was one less than 1000. Stuart suggested multiplying by 1 and Amanda suggested adding 1! Clearly, some work on which operations are associated with different situations is called for with this group. For the time being, I commented that we needed to 'take 1 off'. Katy seemed to latch onto 'take' and pressed the subtract button and the '1'. The children did not know how to read '999' but were excited when told it was nine hundred and ninety-nine.

When asked to look back at their papers, at first Amanda and Stuart thought their results fitted in with the others. Then Amanda realized that there were more spaces than rungs on her 17, 18 example, not the other way round. This prompted checking the other results on these two children's pages and each was found to differ similarly from the first set of results. The children seemed mystified! I asked Christopher to count the number of rungs and spaces in Amanda's smallest ladder: he made it 3 rungs and 2 spaces. Amanda was very indignant, claiming that she could see that the 4 spaces was right. When she then pointed to them in turn, Christopher realized that she was counting them differently from him. I asked Stuart how he had set about his and he realized that he had been counting differently from Katy, Michael and Christopher too. I stressed that no one was wrong in their method of counting: each person had a sensible idea and had correct 'answers' for their own rule. We just had to be careful not to expect the numbers to agree if we put together different ways of obtaining the results.

Case study: machine combinations

I showed a group of 7 year olds a diagram like the one in figure 4.12 and said that we were going to pretend that it was two machines put together, one a "multiply by 2" machine and the other an "add 1" machine. I asked the children which number would come out if 5 were put in. They were quick to decide on 11. Then I gave them each a copy of the outline of the 'machines' and asked them to choose their own numbers to feed into them, and to work out what would come out.

Figure 4.12

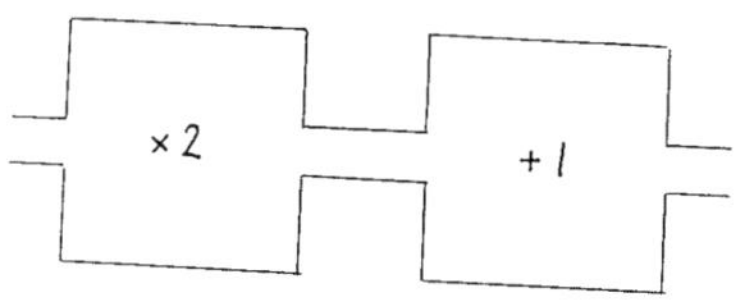

They set about the task without difficulty and were able to carry on on their own. Tuesday chose four small numbers (2, 4, 3, 8) to go through her machine whilst Paul chose two small ones (3, 6) and two rather more ambitious ones (12, 14). Warren started at 7 then chose consecutive numbers going backwards, that is 6, 5 and 4. He was interested to find that there was a pattern in the results: he wrote 'It keeps on going down in twos.' Scott started at 6, then chose increasing consecutive numbers (7, 8, 9, 10, 11, 12). He noticed that four of the numbers had 1s in the tens and three had 2s in the tens and that all the answers were odd numbers. See figures 4.13 and 4.14 for examples of the work.

Figure 4.13

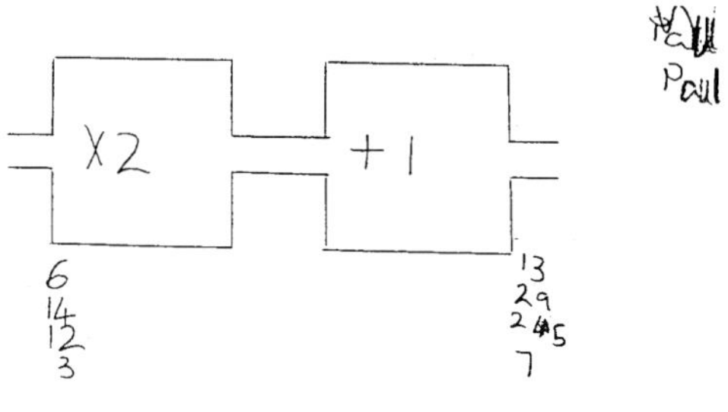

Figure 4.14

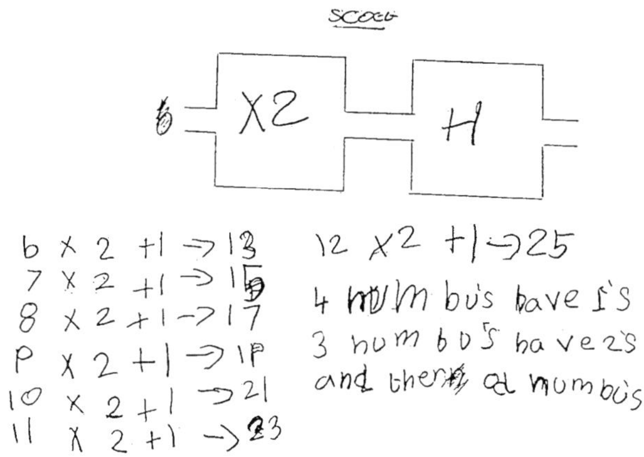

Having asked the children to talk about what they had done and noticed, I then invited them to choose their own operations for a combination of two machines and to try out putting numbers through them.

Scott chose x11, +1 and saw what happened to four increasing consecutive numbers starting from 9. He used a calculator to help with the arithmetic, as did the other three children for this second part of the activity. Scott noticed that there were 'double numbers' at the 'end' of each of his answers. See figure 4.15.

Figure 4.15

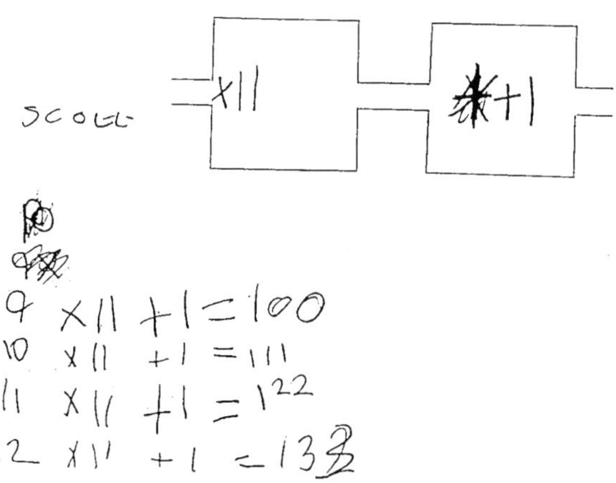

Paul chose x 3, - 2 and fed in eight numbers, including some quite large examples. See figure 4.16

Figure 4.16

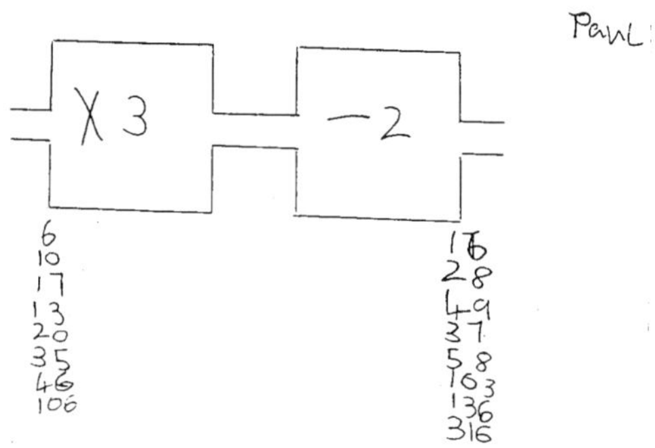

Warren chose x 5, + 3 and fed in seven numbers which started at 10 and decreased consecutively as in his first example. After he had completed working on the input of 6, he announced that the numbers went in a pattern. Pointing to the units he read out '3, 8, 3, 8, 3'. I said that perhaps he could predict ahead for the next number, then. He predicted 28 correctly and was very pleased when he worked out that this was right. He also predicted and checked the result for the next number too. See figure 4.17.

Figure 4.17

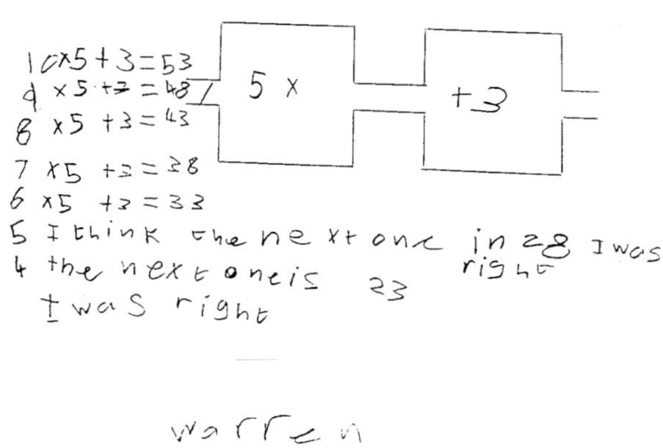

Tuesday chose x 10, + 6. For her first three numbers she picked 2, 5 and 8. It was probably an accident that these happened to be in a pattern, but I commented to her on them going up in threes and said perhaps she might like to continue that idea, knowing that she would obtain a pattern in her results too. This she did for four more numbers and was delighted to find that the results each ended in 6. It would have been interesting to have seen if she could have worked out the differences between the numbers too. See figure 4.18

Figure 4.18

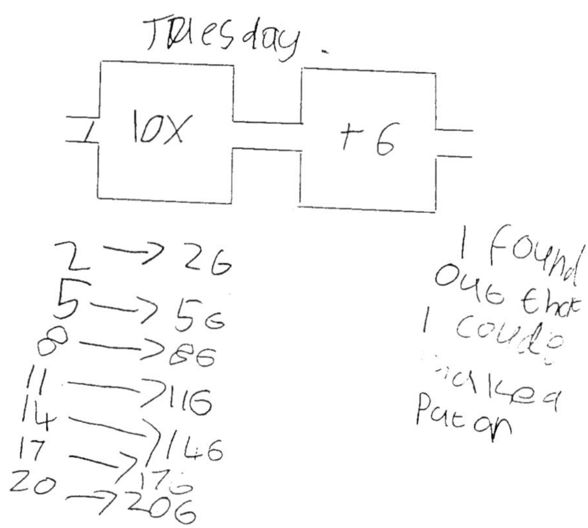

Chapter 5: Missing numbers

Gappy arithmetic

Children often become fixed on the idea that one can only find the number on the right hand side of an addition sum.(1) Having practised lots of examples, they may be confident tackling sums such as

a) 4 + 5 =
10 + 2 =

but be totally thrown by ones such as

b) ■+ 2 = 9
3 +❑= 6

or

c) ❑= 2 + 5
8 = 4 + ?

in which they have to find the missing numbers. But it is important for children to become conversant with this sort of situation, as such representation is an important facet of the concepts of 'addition' and 'equivalence'. Moreover, finding the missing numbers can draw attention to the links between addition and subtraction: one way of finding which number needs to be added to 2 to give 9 is, of course, to subtract 2 from 9.

One fruitful way of involving pupils in tackling such sums is to invite them to make up some additions then mess up one of the numbers on the left hand side. Other children can then try to work out which number has been 'smudged'. Children often seem to be able to relate to this idea. When symbols such as ■ or * or even, say, 's' are subsequently introduced, they can first be thought of as being 'in place of the smudge' and hence do not seem so remote. At the beginning, it is important to encourage children to say the statements in words: 'Three add a smudged number equals ten" etc. This can help considerably towards making their structure evident.

As with so many situations, children can be invited to make up their own examples of additions or subtractions in which a number has to be found to fit in a box or replace a star etc. See figure 5.1 for 7 year old Robert's attempts at this. His examples were far more complicated than those originally given to him to solve!

Involving children in sums of types b) and c) above, also sews some seeds for them starting to see that symbols can be used to stand for unknown numbers. The introduction to algebraic notation is a notorious stumbling block for many children.

But potential problems in Key Stages 2 and 3 can be eased considerably if children are involved in meaningful situations where they use symbols informally within other number work within Key Stage 1. The following four activities incorporate an informal use of symbols whilst involving children in further aspects of the understanding of early number.

Figure 5.1

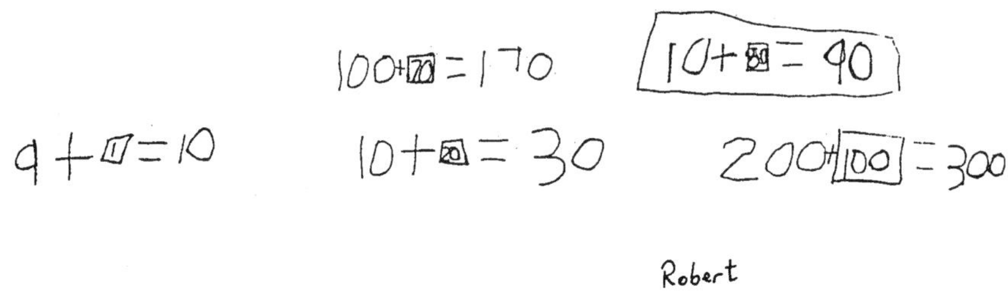

Ladders

This is a version of the traditional snakes and ladders game but without any snakes and, instead of using a normal die, the children throw a cube on which 1, 2 and 3 appear on three faces and a star (or some other symbol) appears on each of the other three faces. The idea is that, if a child throws a star, she can decide which of the numbers 1 to 6 the star stands for and move that number of spaces. Not only does this involve children in thinking of a symbol as standing for a number, it can also involve them in planning which is an appropriate number to choose each time.

To start with, children will often choose 6 as the number of spaces provided by a star, presumably thinking that this will take them the furthest. However, before long, someone normally realizes that it is better to aim for the bottom of a ladder and hence work out which number will take the counter to that place. Sometimes there are two possible ladders to aim for and this provides something else for the children to take into account: it is not necessarily choosing a number which will take the counter to the first ladder which is the best move, it is sensible to look beyond it to see if there are any better possibilities. Deciding on the best choice of numbers in such circumstances can be quite complicated for many young children to tackle. This is why it seems sensible not to have snakes as well as ladders on the board, at least at first.

A case study of children playing the ladders game is given at the end of the last chapter. See also the first of the two case studies at the end of the last chapter for a description of a follow-up activity.

A matching game

This game utilizes a set of playing cards with numerals written on them, some with just one numeral, others with two or more. The following seem to work well, but obviously lots of other variations are possible:

Three each of 1, 2, 3, 4, 5, 6, 7;

Seven pairs such as 1, 5; 1, 7; 2, 3; 2, 4; 2, 5; 3, 4; 3, 6;

One each of a set of three, four, five and six numerals, for example 1, 6, 7; 1, 2, 4, 5; 1, 2, 3, 4, 5; 1, 2, 3, 4, 5, 6;

Twelve cards with a symbol, such as a diamond, on each.

The idea of the game is for a small group of children, say four, to have four cards each and take it in turns placing a card on top of a previous card, with the rule that if the new card has numerals on it, at least one of them must match one of the numerals on the previous card. Suppose, for example, that the last card played is 3, 4. Then the next player could play any card which contains a 3 or a 4 or both, say, 2, 3 or 3 or 1, 2, 4, 5 etc. A diamond can be played at any time and the player states the number it will represent. This can be any number within the set 1 to 7, not necessarily one of the ones on the previous card. The player calls out 'the diamond is a ___' and play continues. If at any time a player cannot go at all, then he takes a card from the top of the unused stack to see if that could be used. If not, he has to miss a go. Play continues until a child has no cards left.

The rules sound complicated, but children seem to find them easy enough to pick up when actually shown how to play.[2] It is often helpful to play with the pack without the diamonds at first so that the matching rule can be focused on and understood. Also, this means that the game is likely to become 'stuck' and the diamonds are then a welcome addition to the available cards because of the extra choices they bring.

Children seem to find the use of the diamonds appealing and enjoy having them in their hands of cards. Sometimes, individuals choose numbers beyond 1 to 7 for the value of the diamond, for example Alison (5 years) chose 8 at one point. In some cases this could be because the children are unaware that the particular number chosen does not lie between 1 and 7. Other children are likely to spot the problem, however, because no one will be able to go next unless they place another diamond.

Other children only use the diamond cards when they cannot use any others. In fact, this is a sensible strategy, but they probably do not see it as a strategy at all. How can we make them aware of alternatives and then to decide on 'best' moves?

Adding to 10

This game utilizes a set of playing cards with the numerals 1 to 9 written on them. Six each of the numerals seems to work well for a group of four children. There are also twelve extra cards with a symbol written on each of them.

The game is played as follows: Each child is dealt six of the cards. In turn, each child puts down a pair of cards whose numerals add to 10, if he has such a pair, and replenishes his hand by picking up two more cards from the stock pile. A symbol can be used to stand for any number. If someone cannot go, then he picks up an extra card from the pile, sees if 10 can be made now, but if not, has to wait until his next turn to try again. The game continues until there are no more cards in the stock pile. The winner is the child who has collected the most pairs of 10.

At some point, children might discover that they have a set of three (or more) cards in their hand which add to 10 and ask if they can put them all down. As a group, thay could make their own decision about this. If they allow the more-than-two-cards situation, then they could also discuss whether it is best to count the number of pairs, triples etc. at the end, or to count the total numbr of cards each has turned over.

As with the matching game, it seems helpful if children play the game without the symbol cards first, so that the adding-to-10 rule can be focused on by itself at the beginning.

An extension would be to aim for numbers other than 10 as totals. If a different total is adopted, children could think whether the numbers on the cards themselves should also be changed. They might also be asked how the game could be altered to involve subtraction as well as addition.

As well as being a useful and interesting activity in its own right, the game can be used as a lead in to children solving such statements as $8 + \blacksquare = 10$, $n + 3 = 10$ etc.

A case study of children playing the game is given at the end of this chapter.

Coded squares

A class of 7/8 year olds had worked out how to make a 3 x 3 magic square with the numbers 4,4,4,5,5,5,6,6,6, also with 3,3,3,5,5,5,7,7,7. When asked to think very hard for a little while of anything they could try next, one of the ideas was that letters could be used instead of numbers, like in a code. Stacey, the originator of the idea, and some other children went on to produce some examples like this. See figure 5.2 for Stacey's work and Bird (1986), chapter 5, for more details. Later, the idea was taken further with different children substituting numbers of their own choices for Stacey's letters and seeing what happened.

Figure 5.2

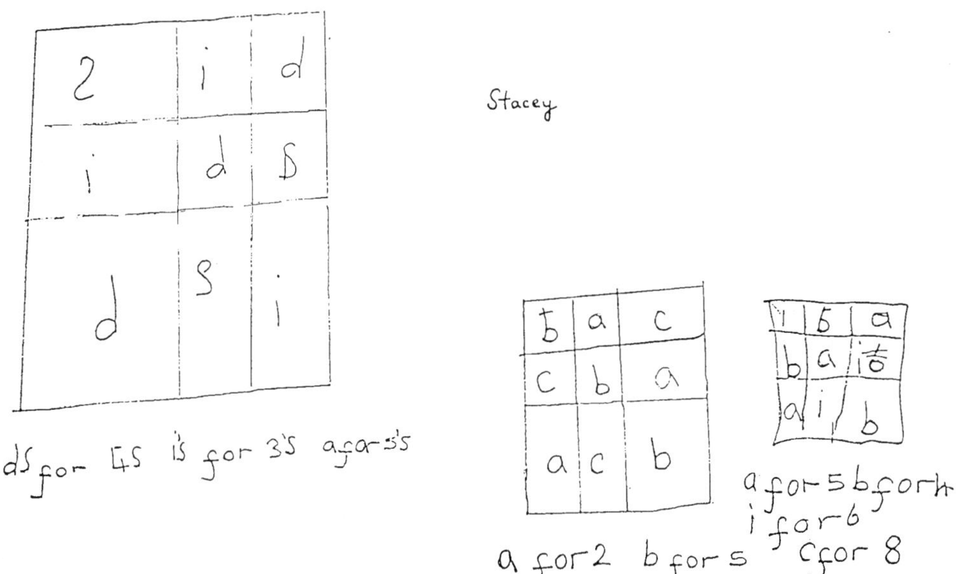

The idea could be used as a starting-point in its own right. Children could be shown, say,

r d n
n r d
d n r

and invited to put numbers in for the letters, the same number each time the letter is the same. See, for example, 6 year old Richard's work in figure 5.3. They could investigate the totals of the rows, columns and diagonals and try to find some values for d, n, r for which all the totals are the same.

Figure 5.3

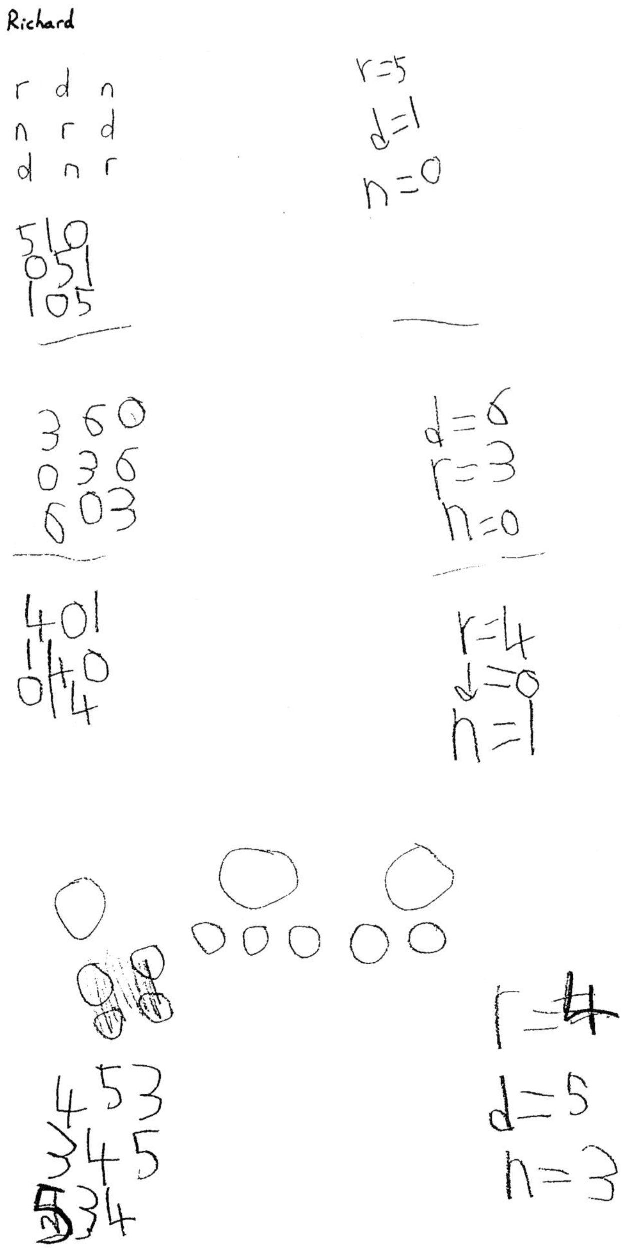
Richard
r d n
n r d
d n r
r=5
d=1
n=0
510
051
105
360
036
603
d=6
r=3
n=0
401
140
014
r=4
d=0
n=1
453
345
534
r=4
d=5
n=3

Gappy sequences

Ask the children to start with a number, say 2, and to count on from that in, say 3s, giving in this case 2, 5, 8, 11, 14 ... Write down the sequence in front of the children, then cover up one of the numbers: who can say which number is missing?

The children can then be asked to choose their own starting number each, secretly, and a number to keep on adding on by. Once they have produced a series of several numbers they can then block out one of them, swop papers with a neighbour and try to work out each other's missing number. This presents a greater challenge than the teacher's example because, when working out each other's examples, the children will have to determine what was being added on each time. Also, some children are likely to choose more complicated numbers than the teacher's original ones to begin the sequence and add on by.

Some children may guess at the missing number instead of trying to work it out. This could be discouraged by the children receiving points for correct answers, say 3 points if the first number they suggest is correct, but only say 1 point for the second attempt. The greater number of points for a number-right-first-time might provide an incentive to try to use some reasoning rather than sheer guesswork. It would also turn the activity into more of a game.

Inevitably, some children will make mistakes when actually producing their own sequence of numbers. If a child's partner spots a mistake, the partner could gain, say, 3 points herself automatically. Or the children could decide on similar penalties themselves.

The National Curriculum

The activities discussed in this chapter all address the idea of 'understanding the use of a symbol to stand for an unknown number', that is, part of Attainment Target 3 (Algebra), level 2. 'Talking about their work and asking questions' (Attainment Target 1: Using and applying mathematics, level 1) is likely to feature highly too.

Opportunities are also provided for other parts of the Attainment Targets to feature in particular activities. As examples:

> The matching game (p. 103) incorporates the idea of recognizing numerals and knowing which numbers are less than 7. It thus links with 'counting, reading, writing and ordering numbers to at least 10', that is A.T.2 (Number), level 1.
>
> A lot of addition is likely to occur in the adding to 10 game (p. 104) and the activity should help children learn and practise number bonds to 10. This links with 'knowing and using addition and subtraction facts up to 10' (A.T.2, level 2). More addition is inevitable in the coded squares activity. Children might well choose numbers over 10 to replace the letters and hence opportunities are

provided for involvement in 'Learning and using addition and subtraction facts to 20' (A.T.2, level 3).

The dice throwing ladders game (p. 110) might well involve children in 'recognizing that there is a degree of uncertainty about the outcomes of some events' (A.T.5: Handling data, level 2). Moving correctly along the rows of numbers on the board will involve children in thinking about the order of the numbers and hence in 'reading, writing and ordering numbers to at least 100' (A.T.2, level 2).

THE NATIONAL CURRICULUM FOR KEY STAGE 1 MATHEMATICS

The 'Gappy arithmetic' activity (p. 107) will involve children in extending their ideas about addition and equivalence, which links with relating 'numerals and other mathematical symbols, eg. '+', '=', to a range of situations' (Using and Applying Mathematics: 3b). There will also be opportunities for connecting the concepts of addition and subtraction which links with developing 'a variety of methods for adding and subtracting, including using the fact that subtraction is the inverse of addition' (Number: 3d) and 'understand the operations of addition, subtraction as taking away and comparison, and the relationship between them' (from Number: 4a). The children will also be involved in the use of 'addition and subtraction facts to 20' (from Number: 3c).

Moving correctly along the rows of numbers on the board in the 'Ladders' game (p. 110) will involve children in reading some of the numbers and thinking about their order, which links with 'read, write and order numbers' from

Number: 2b. The children will carry out some simple counting (up to 6) when moving their counters along the board (part of Number: 2a). When choosing a number to replace a star, children can be asked to give reasons for their choice, hence requiring them to 'explain their thinking to support the development of their reasoning' (Using and Applying Mathematics: 1b).

The 'Matching game' (p.103) incorporates the idea of recognising numerals and knowing which numbers are less than 7. It thus links with 'read, write and order numbers initially to 10' from Number: 2b.

A lot of addition is likely to occur in the 'Adding to 10' game (p. 110) and the activity should help children learn and practise number bonds to 10. This is part of 'know addition and subtraction facts to 20' (from Number: 3c) and connects with 'understand the operations of addition, ...' (from Number: 4a). More addition is inevitable in the 'Coded squares' activity (p. 104), involving both Number: 3c and Number: 4a again. This latter activity also provides opportunities for children to 'recognise simple patterns' (part of Using and Applying Mathematics: 4a) and 'use repeating patterns' (from Number: 3a).

In the Gappy sequences' activity (p. 107), the children will be required to 'count in steps of different sizes' and 'recognise sequences' (part of Number: 2a). Working out which numbers are missing is likely to involve some notion of order (what can be between, say, 8 and 14?) and addition, hence parts of Number: 2b, 3c and 4a will be relevant.

Case study: ladders game

I showed a group of five 6/7 year olds some boards as depicted in figure 5.4. The children realized that the boards were like 'snakes and ladders' and laughed about there not being any snakes! I gave one of the boards to Christopher and Stuart, together with two counters and a die made up from an originally blank wooden cube on which had been written the numbers 1, 2 and 3 once each and a star * three times. Amanda, Richard and Katy had another board, die and counters. Each little group started playing immediately, obviously being very familiar with the usual snakes and ladders game.

Katy was the first to throw a star, or a 'cross' as she called it. The children had not paid any attention to what was on the dice before using them and were now surprised and amused to find that they were different from usual. I said that whoever threw a star could pretend it was whichever number they liked from 1 to 6. The children seemed quite excited by this.

Katy chose six for her first star. The other children chose sixes several times too, presumably because throwing a six is often considered the best score in an ordinary dice game. Christopher, however, immediately saw that he could choose a number which would land him at the foot of a ladder. He kept on using this strategy and so became far ahead of Stuart and, indeed, far ahead of the children playing on the other board. Gradually, the others seemed to appreciate the idea and started to use it themselves. In their second game, all of the children used the strategy at some point.

After a while, Christopher also realized that sometimes there was potential for reaching more than one ladder within one throw of the die. In such cases, he worked out which ladder would lead him furthest up the board, then worked out the appropriate number to stand for his star.

Some of the children wanted to be able to go up a ladder if their counter landed in the middle of it. Other children were adamant that this was 'not fair'. Some children found it difficult to follow the order of the numbers on the board, particularly when they had just gone up a ladder and therefore were not following a direction along a row already. I encouraged the children to keep an eye on each others' moves to help sort out the correct pathways. This seemed to work quite well.

By the time the children were playing their third games, it was evident that they were well into trying to think ahead to choose the best possible number on throwing a star. They made comments about each others' moves too. Remarks such as 'If he says "four" he can go up the ladder' (Amanda) became commonplace.

A variation on the game would be to have a die with no numbers at all on it, but two different symbols, say a cross and a circle. Each time a child throws a cross, say, she could choose a number, but everytime she throws a circle her opponent would choose the number of moves for her (the thrower) to move forward. It might be fun to include snakes as well as ladders on the board for this game.

Figure 5.4

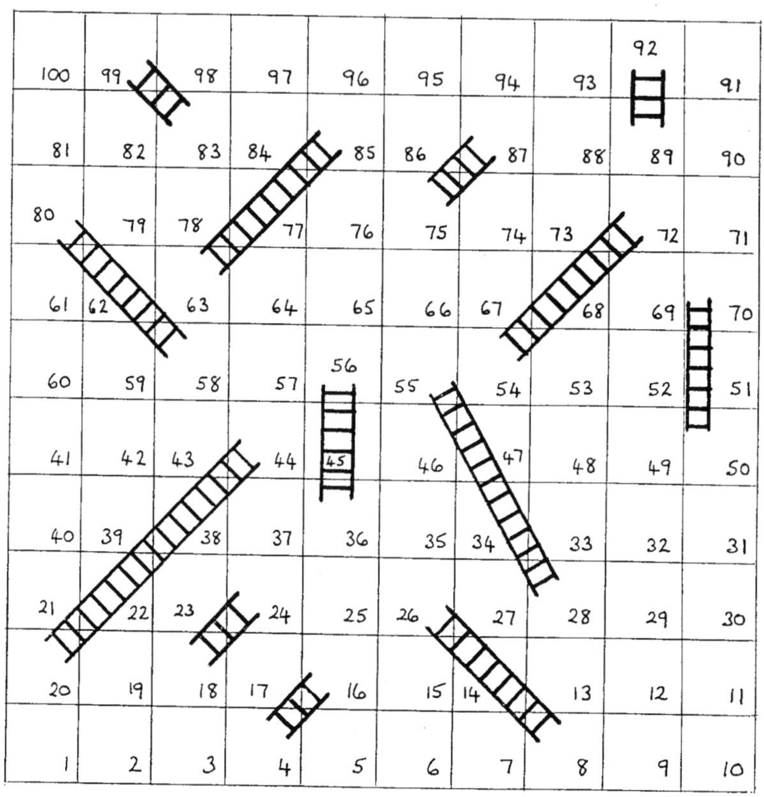

Case study: Adding to 10 game

For this activity, cards were used as described on p. 104, that is fifty-four cards comprising six each of the numbers from 1 to 9 and twelve cards with symbols written on them. In this particular case, the symbols were letters: a,a,a,a,m,m,m,m,p,p,p,p. This was to see how the children reacted to using letters to stand for numbers. The repetition of letters (four ms etc.) was to provide opportunities for children to see that the same letter could be used to stand for a different number on a different occasion.

To start with, each of a group of four 6/7 year olds were dealt six of the number cards each. I asked the children to put their cards face uppermost so that we could all help each other out at the beginning. Neil was interested in who had the highest card and found that Marie and Michelle both had 9s.

I asked each child to see if he or she had a pair of cards which added to 10. Going round the group in turn, each child put their pair down if they found one, then replenished their hand by picking up two more cards from the stock pile. The pair was turned over and kept by the child who had selected them. If someone could not go, then he or she picked up an extra card from the pile, saw if 10 could be made now and, if not, had to miss the turn.

Neil was very quick at deciding on pairs of numbers which added to 10. It was interesting to see how others seemed to increase their speed of recognition of some pairs as the game progressed, presumably learning from working out the pairings themselves earlier, or learning from each other.

When it was her turn at one point, Marie could not see a way of making 10 with two numbers but she asked me if she could use three. She had worked out that the 5, 3 and 2 which she had in her hand, added to 10. I asked the rest of the children what they thought and they agreed that it was all right. This then became an accepted part of the rules, used by the others too.

The game stopped when there were no more cards in the stock pile and when the group had exhausted the sums to 10 on the cards in their hands. The children were keen to see who had managed to turn the most cards over. They counted them and found it was Marie.

The group were eager to play the game again. I said that this time, however, there would be some new cards in the pack. They were very amused to find that these extra cards had letters on them and said the sound of each of the letters. I said that if they had a letter in their hand they could pretend that it was any number that they liked. This idea seemed to appeal to them.

Michelle dealt out the cards. I suggested that the children had just four cards each this time because, otherwise, perhaps they might always be able to go?

The children coped immediately with using the letters. So that they did not merely put them down blindly, I encouraged them to say which number a letter stood for each time they used one.

Mark, Neil and Marie knew some number pairs straight off. For example, Marie put down 8 and m at one point, announcing immediately that m would be 2. Michelle had to keep working out what the letters would have to stand for. For example, at one point, when she put down 2 and p she counted on her fingers to find that p would have to be 8.

Mark was the first to decide to use three cards including a letter. Others then followed. So here were the children, needing to work out what the letters would have to stand for by adding the other two cards and then finding their total's complement in 10. Quite an achievement for 6/7 year olds!

It was also interesting to see that the children seemed unconcerned by the same letter being used for different numbers at different points. And it was exciting to see that Neil used a and m both together at one point. He said that one was 2 and the other was 8. At the end, I referred back to this event, asking the children which other pairs of numbers the a and m could have been. Together they were able to exhaust the possibilities.

Notes

1. Some sensitive points about this problem are made in 'Language and Mathematics', produced by the Association of Teachers of Mathematics; 1980. See pp. 32-35. See also Behr M., Erlwanger S. and Nichols E.; How children view the equals sign; Mathematics Teaching No.92; September 1980.

2. Indeed, inspiration for this game came from watching a 3 year old absorbed in playing something rather similar but with pictures instead of numbers and symbols. This was one of Waddington's games: 'Thomas the Tank Engine and Friends'; Kaye and Ward Ltd; 1985.

3. For some groups of children, it might be sensible to have arrows on the board to indicate the direction of moves, or the trail could even look more like a zig-zag path as in figure 5.5. In these cases, however, the children would not have to consider the order of the numerals at all, indeed he numerals become irrelevant.

Figure 5.5

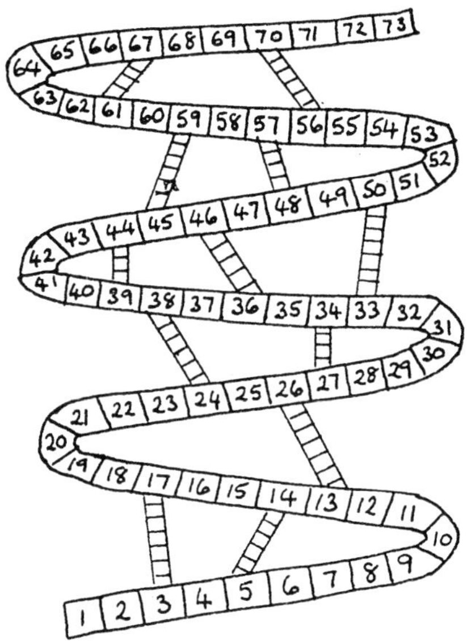

References and resources

Texts

Association of Teachers of Mathematics (1977), Notes on mathematics for children, Cambridge: Cambridge University Press.

Association of Teachers of Mathematics (1980), Language and Mathematics, Nelson: Association of Teachers of Mathematics.

Association of Teachers of Mathematics (1986), 102, Derby: Association of Teachers of Mathematics.

Atkinson, S. (ed) (1992), Mathematics with reason: the emergent approach to primary mathematics, London: Hodder and Stoughton.

Behr, M., Erlwanger, S., and Nichols, E. (1980), 'How children view the equals sign', Mathematics Teaching 92.

Bird, M.H. (1986), Mathematics with seven and eight year olds, Leicester: The Mathematical Association.

Bird, M.H. (1987), Openings: some ideas which have been used with four and five year olds to stimulate mathematical activity, West Sussex Institute of Higher Education.

Bird, M.H. (1991), Mathematics for young children: an active thinking approach, London: Routledge.

Blinko, J. and Graham, N. (1988), Mathematical beginnings: problem solving for young children, Colchester: Claire Publications.

Charbonneau, M.N. (1975), Hidden rods/ hidden numbers, New York: Cuisenaire Company of America.

Department of Education and Science (1995), Mathematics in the National Curriculum, London: HMSO.

Gattegno, C. (1957), Mathematics with numbers in colour, Reading: Educational Explorers Ltd.

Gattegno, C. (1963), For the teaching of mathematics (Volumes 1, 2, and 3), Reading: Educational Explorers Ltd.

Goutard, M. (1964), Mathematics and children, Reading: Educational Explorers Ltd.

Mason, J. (1990), Algebra (part of Supporting primary mathematics), PM649S, Milton Keynes: The Open University.

Oxfordshire Mathematics Centre (1991), Activities towards algebra targets, Oxfordshire County Council.

Oxfordshire Mathematics Centre (1996), Number patterns and relationships, Oxfordshire Quality Schools Association.

Woodman, A. and Albany, E. (1988), Mathematics through art and design 6 - 13, London: Unwin Hyman.

Other sources

Multi-link Activity Cards, in particular Number Activity Cards sets SY347 and SY348; Pattern Cards SY563, SY564, SY565, and SY566, from E.J. Arnold.

'Pressure mat' microcomputer programs by R. and P. Phillips from Panthera, 1990.

Project File on 'Pattern' in Child Education, Vol.68, No.11, 1991.

'A series of discs for creative work in mathematics' by D.V. Smith obtainable from the Mathematics Centre, Chichester Institute of Higher Education.

The Vol.1, No.3 (1991) edition of Strategies: Maths and problem solving 3 - 13, is devoted to the theme of 'pattern'.

Index